LIVING AND LEARNING IN PEACE AND WAR

JO VELLACOTT

Living and Learning in Peace and War

Jo Vellacott

SPOKESMAN
Nottingham

First published in 2018 by
Spokesman
Russell House
Bulwell Lane
Nottingham NG6 0BT
UK

Phone 0115 9708318
www.spokesmanbooks.com

A catalogue record is available from the British Library

ISBN 978 0 85124 870 7

Printed and bound in Nottingham by Russell Press
www.russellpress.com

Contents

Introduction and Acknowledgements

When you live as long as I have, the early years of your life gradually morph into a historical period, remembered by few, but read about by some. Probably, for me, an added consciousness comes from my own experience as a historian.

Even to me, the 1920s seem strange, so different from anything we know now. I have not tried to portray society in any large way, and am just hoping to convey something of the flavour of a particular culture at a particular time, and of my own growth in and beyond that culture, with its (and my) deficits and blessings. This is a very personal story: it is also a small piece of social history.

A complete list of those whose input was essential to the writing of this book would surely have to include almost all of those mentioned in it, even the worthy but regrettably unloved governess, Miss Straw, who taught me to write English. My parents and Nannie, who feature largely in the text, also took it for granted that I would write. More recent help and encouragement has come from so many people that I am sure I shall leave out many who deserve a mention, although I am of necessity keeping it to those who have in some way helped in the writing of this book, rather than straying into the very wide field of those who have made the story it tells worth telling.

First among those who have given exceptional skilled professional help in editing – and encouragement, and in so many other ways – is my daughter, Mary Newberry. All my family has given amazing support, practical and moral. My son-out-law, Rory Gus Sinclair, has encouraged me to tell my stories, and has fed me with many wonderful gourmet dinners. My son, Douglas Newberry (with his wife, Irene England), supports me in many ways, and deserves special mention for his generous contribution to my technology, both in the form of up-to-date hardware and of patient tuition in the needed skills. From time to time, my daughter, Soo, has also been there for me with loving encouragement.

At an early stage, my friend Jean Dean transformed many pages of difficult handwriting into a neat, legible typed manuscript, the bones of this final version. Before that, there was my friend Ellie Segel, with whom I once drove across Canada to a Quaker Meeting; she always felt time was wasted if she was not doing at least three things at once, so she took along a tape recorder and had me tell my life story along the way. Later, she lived with me for a while before her death from cancer, and spent long hours transcribing it all on to my computer.

Help with specific enquiries has been generously given by Robin Darwall-Smith, Graham Naylor, Celia Gibbs and Giles Craven.

Elly Parry deserves special mention for her informative PowerPoint biography of my good friend her great grandmother, Felicity Craven (nee Avern).

Some of the illustrations by my own inexpert hand owe a great deal to encouragement and help from Chantal Gobeil, whose art classes so well addressed the need of older students, regardless of previous experience and skill.

Warm thanks go to the Downe House Seniors Association for providing financial assistance and encouragement.

I greatly appreciate the support and help I have had from Tony Simpson and Nicole Morris at Spokesman Press.

Jo V
Toronto, 2017

CHAPTER 1

Birth and Background

I have always supposed, I am sure rightly, that my birth was a welcome event. My parents having married late, our family was one of the smaller branches of my father's large clan. But in my generation girls were quite scarce, seemingly limited to one per nuclear family, whether the total number of children was four, five, six, or (as in our case) three, of whom I was the youngest. My parents already had two sons, and there were unlikely to be more after me. I may have worn out my welcome quite quickly, but welcome I do not doubt there was.

This did not make it any easier to choose a name for me. Harold, my father, might have liked me called Josephine after my mother, or Ruth after his favourite sister, but Jo (as my mother was called) wanted to keep her monopoly of the former, and perhaps did not share his view of her sister-in-law. For whatever reason, they were still debating the matter some days after my birth. Harold was sitting in Jo's room while she continued the leisurely recovery from childbirth enjoyed in those days by the English middle class. He was playing a game of patience, a lifelong refuge from stress for him, and one which I inherited from him.

When Jo exclaimed, not for the first time, 'Harold, what are we to call this child?' he answered, without looking up, 'Oh, call her Patience!' to which she replied, 'All right, I will!'

But after all of it, the whole negotiation was in vain. They ended up by giving me all three of the names, Patience Josephine Ruth, and then rejecting use of all. The first by common consent was considered disastrously inappropriate (for who was to know that I was named after a card game, not the virtue on which I at once fell short?). My mother banned the usual diminutive 'Jo' of the second because that was how she was known. My brother, George, two and a half years older than myself, made his own, 'Jo'phine'. And this was what I was called until I went to boarding school, when my mother's prohibition was withdrawn, and I became Jo to my contemporaries. Sometimes I think Ruth is rather a likeable name, but it is too late to turn myself into a Ruth now. And sometimes I regret the loss of Jo'phine, which was mine and mine alone. But Jo will do, and fifty or sixty years later I managed to more or less officially shed all the rest, along with a different surname I had carried for a number of years.

Once I was born, my parents were not the most important people in my daily life, though I soon knew that they were to be treated as such. For the first month, I must have been under the direction of my mother and the monthly nurse. Between them, they probably got me bound into the routines considered so important in those days. I do remember hearing that I had been 'a colicky baby', which may mean that I was resistant to the routines. All that month, I suspect, Nannie had been waiting anxiously

Jo'phine with toy baby carriage

in the wings, and of course looking after Douglas and George. She took over my care with love and delight as soon as she was allowed and to the extent allowed – in other words, as far as strict adherence to the norms of regularity of sleeping, eating and defecating permitted.

My parents had started married life with scant means, rising during my postwar childhood to a comfortable professional level, enhanced perhaps by the need to present a more than respectable appearance, complete with servants, to the professional colleagues and patients who came regularly to the house. Harold was the youngest of twelve children of an Essex 'gentleman farmer'. After indifferent private schooling and a hated spell as a clerk in some office, Harold had made a late start to fulfil his dream of becoming a surgeon. He studied at the London Hospital in the East End as, in effect, an apprentice. There was plenty of book work and classroom instruction, but he never went to university as we know it, though the hospital must have been affiliated with London University.

Harold's family

He had lived at home except when on call, and travelled to and from Essex daily by train. Once he won a small monetary prize for excellence in anatomy, and used it to buy a first- or perhaps second-class season ticket so that he could be sure of a seat, to make studying on his journey easier than it was in a crowded third-class carriage. His father was gravely displeased by what he saw as Harold's self-indulgence and putting on airs. After he got his MD, he stayed on for several years doing a sequence of resident's jobs at the London Hospital. Finally, some time after he was awarded his Fellowship in the Royal College of Surgeons, he proposed to my mother, Josephine Sempill. She was then a senior nurse at Poplar Hospital, where the work was mainly with accident victims. In 1913, they got married and made the move to Devonshire. I do not think Harold had ever liked London, nor had he the needed capital to set up there. Whether his choice of the West Country owed anything to the Devonshire origins of our name and family I do not know – only in my grandfather's generation had the Vellacotts decided to multiply in Essex – but it was a good choice.

Jo had had a very difficult time at the beginning of the war. Harold's surgical practice in Devonport was scarcely on its feet when war broke out. He was in the reserve and left almost immediately for the Royal Medical Corps, leaving Jo pregnant with their first baby. She was well over thirty years old, considered at that time late for a first birth, and indeed she seems to have had a rough time. Harold, at the Front, was given the news that neither mother nor child might survive; both did. Jo was at heart something of a mischievous freethinking Scot. Her happiness was not enhanced by the caring but disapproving attention given her by Harold's Plymouth Brethren family, with whom she lived for the first months of the war and who were as much concerned – perhaps more – to save her soul as to look after her physical health, let alone her happiness. Being prayed over can be a bit of a put-down.

By the time my brother Douglas was eleven months old, she had managed to return to Devonport and her own household. She advertised for a nursemaid to train, and the sixteen-year-old Bertha Cruze was the successful applicant. Bertha remained with our family for more than fifty years. Shortly after the end of the war, before my birth, the family moved from Devonport into Plymouth, where Harold obtained appointments as consultant at the general hospitals in Plymouth and Tavistock, and later also at several outlying 'cottage hospitals'.

When I read that wonderful book *Lark Rise to Candleford*, I thought how close the picture it painted must be to Nannie's background. I wished I had known of it in time to give her a copy. She was a great reader and would have loved it. Born Bertha Cruze, one of six children living with hardworking parents in a small country cottage well outside a small village, she had been apprenticed to a dressmaker at the age of twelve. The law allowed for children to leave school at that age if they were to be trained in a trade, and she was very grateful to her parents for having had the forethought and found the money for her apprenticeship fee. It was only in passing and because I questioned her that I found out that she had left home at seven every morning for the two years of the apprenticeship. She had walked the two miles to the small town where the dressmaker's shop was located, and had worked six days a week for – as I remember it – ten hours, with two fifteen minute breaks and a half hour for lunch.

But she had been well taught, and had enjoyed the company of the other apprentices, even if they worked under a stern if kindly discipline that permitted no time for gossip or play. The contract had been kept with integrity on both sides; her training was thorough and she emerged with a full complement of dressmaking skills. She applied these with art and a meticulous attention to detail. At age fourteen, her apprenticeship complete, she obtained a resident post as 'children's maid' to two well-off girls, one aged sixteen, the other of her own age. A children's maid was the stepping stone to being a lady's maid, and with her qualifications, she seemed set to do well, though probably always in domestic service.

Later, as a historian with a particular interest in the time of the First World War, I had the curious experience of recognising that little bits of my own memories were significant tessera of a mosaic that would later form a picture that I would meet again in the work of social historians, and would indeed refer to in my own work. I recognised Nannie as one of many who lost their jobs on the outbreak of the First World War. The upper classes cut back on expenses by discharging what came to be considered unnecessary servants, and by dispensing with dressmakers, who were thrown out of work by the hundred. Bertha suddenly became a luxury her employers could do without. I even envisage a gleam of satisfaction in the eye of the master of the house as he was able to cut down – in the name of patriotism – on what he had long seen as the extravagance of his womenfolk.

So Bertha was discharged, and shortly was hired by Jo. When I was born, Bertha, now and forever after known to us as Nannie, had already been with my family for nearly seven years, since my older brother, Douglas, born in November 1914, was about a year old. She was very young for a nannie, and had none of the sophisticated training of the nannies we sometimes saw around in uniforms – 'Norland Nurses', I think they were. Her excellent qualifications as a dressmaker seem hardly relevant to the care of a baby, but she was a good learner, and my mother taught her the skills she didn't have. And above all, Nannie brought to her task youth, all the right instincts (moderating those rigidities with which my parents soon indoctrinated her), and a wealth of love, patience, intelligence and understanding. We were extraordinarily blessed to have her.

As a thoroughly up-to-date nurse, recently retired from a senior position, my mother, I am sure, made herself familiar with current wisdom regarding the rearing of children. Much of it, alas, consisted of rules and regimens; we were fed strictly by the clock, we were toilet-trained almost to the extinction of natural urges, we ate what was put in front of us, we wore what was set out for us in the morning. But somehow, it was not as bad as all that makes it sound. I enjoyed my food; second helpings were always available – which I think may account for my sometimes having found myself sitting in front of a dish of rice pudding, unable to force it down after a hearty first course of beef and Yorkshire pudding. Sometimes I enjoyed my clothes, and occasionally I was even allowed to express an opinion at the stage where samples of cotton material were brought in by my mother to choose which ones would be made up into my summer dresses. I had no idea what a privilege I would later see it as, to have had a skilled dressmaker sewing in my very own nursery. I fidgeted through the trying-on sessions, and I had a marked preference for the rough-and-tumble clothes we wore at play in the back yard, a preference supported by my father, who, despite a near paranoia about harmful bacteria, never allowed our play to be restricted by any need to keep away from natural earthy dirt.

CHAPTER 2

Family, Place and Time

The nursery window was high above a street of solid Georgian houses with big windows and high-ceilinged rooms. From it we could see the normal traffic of a residential area, though the horse-drawn vans carrying bread, milk, and who knows what else would make their deliveries from the back lane. But the postman came to the front door, as did my father's patients, the muffin man rang his bell at tea time on the front street, larger carts with heavier loads passed by, once in a while the knife grinder made his presence known (and sometimes Nannie rushed out to get her scissors sharpened). A highlight was when the hurdy-gurdy man set up his instrument, and the nightmare occasion was one icy day when a horse slipped and fell between the shafts, broke a leg and had to be shot. At dusk the lamplighter came by, with a long pole to touch each street gaslight in turn.

Lockyer Street, the house where I was born, now a small hotel

Lockyer Street led up from the centre of the town to the Hoe, the famous Plymouth Hoe, where Sir Francis Drake had watched the coming of the Spanish Armada, taking time to finish his leisurely game of bowls before going on board his ship to defeat the Spanish Armada – with a little help from God, who 'blew with His winds and they were scattered'. The quotation was right there on the Drake monument on the Hoe, where we walked with Nannie every day. There was also the tall war

15

memorial to those who had died – a scant few years ago – in the First World War, another war in which we understood God had been on our side, though no one explained why, if that were the case, he had allowed the list of names inscribed on every facet of the memorial to be so very, very long.

Many years later, this is how I remembered Plymouth Hoe

Plymouth is by the sea, a port, but it has a rather odd configuration. The centre of the town, the shopping area, the big church, the guildhall, lie low behind a bluff and out of sight of the sea. A friend once told me she had spent a day in Plymouth looking for the sea, which she felt should be downhill, and had never found it. On the top of the bluff is the Hoe, a recreational promenade with a magnificent panorama of Plymouth Sound, Mount Batten to the left, Mount Edgcumbe to the right and three lighthouses in view including – on a clear day – the Eddystone, twenty miles out. Beyond the bluff and down to either side of the Hoe there is a sea-level Old Plymouth, including on the east side, the Citadel of the Napoleonic era, a wonderful marine biological aquarium, and the old town of Plymouth with a number of buildings dating back to when the Mayflower sailed, taking the Pilgrim Fathers to the New World. Directly below the Hoe, when I was a child, there was a public swimming pool (seldom used by us because of the adults' fear of infection), two beaches, pebbly rather than sandy, but blessed with many small pieces of

The Smeaton Tower, lighthouse formerly on the Eddystone Rock, 20 miles out to sea

coloured glass ground smooth by the waves (they were jewels to me), and a pier, with penny slot machines where slender chocolate bars could be obtained – but were very seldom permitted. We walked on the Hoe daily, and occasionally brought our tricycles.

At certain times of the year, all the children on the Hoe were whipping tops; at another time, all were skipping rope; at another all were bowling their wooden hoops; even marbles had their season. In the summer we might watch a Punch and Judy show. Although it now seems to me outrageous that we could never play with the other children we saw (not even those with nannies, surely a certificate of social standing) because our mother did not know their mothers, we still managed to follow the current fashions. We persuaded our mother to provide a hoop or a skipping rope or we took our weekly fourpence or sixpence to the local store to buy a top, and persuaded Nannie to initiate us into its techniques. If we walked on the lower road on a good day, a school of dolphins might leap and plunge their way past us. Walks with Nannie were never dull.

Because it was the way to the Hoe, our street carried a good deal of purposeful pedestrian traffic: children and their parents or their nannies, courting couples in the evening, 'trippers' (later to be known as 'tourists'). And yes, there were plenty of cars, but from our vantage point, the roofs of cars seldom provided much interest.

Harold, my father, had served as a surgeon in a Field Ambulance and had received the Military Cross, with bar (which means he earned it twice over), for tending the wounded under fire. He never spoke of the war, yet he conveyed to me a sense that war was a horror that must never be repeated. His sword, a formal part of officers' uniform, lay around in a pile of junk in his carpentry workroom along with the helmet of a German soldier, rather than hanging in a place of honour. I believe that during the General Strike of 1926 he was told to be prepared, as a reservist, to rejoin an army unit. He couldn't find his puttees (leg protection and part of his uniform); he didn't want anything to do with things military; and he thought the strikers had some right on their side. He went around the house closer to swearing than I ever remember from my mild-mannered father. Whether this is in my memory or from someone else's anecdote I don't know; I was only four in 1926.

I would love to be able to say that our household had no military ambience, but the rawness of the war still hung over us, and alas, a sense of its glories seeped in from the town. On very special occasions we watched a military band from the nursery window; I thought it a great treat. My infant soul was deeply stirred by martial music.

Plymouth, together with its twin sisters, Devonport and Stonehouse, was a military city, and even more, a naval one. It possessed a Marine barracks and a famous Marine band. Sometimes we shared our governess with the children of army or navy officers. Occasionally, we were taken to see the Trooping of the Colours at one of the barracks. Always, come Christmas, we waited hopefully to be invited to the Christmas party at the naval or Marine barracks. One was better in

Plymouth Guildhall before the war

our judgement than the other; I can't now remember which one. Both had long slides that took all my courage to commit to. Both had bran tubs with hidden gifts. The naval one had a water pond with tantalising coins at the bottom – and an electric current to make it a challenge to plunge your hand in and snatch one out, controlled by a sailor who moderated the current for such as me and stepped it up for the big boys. My brother George was charged with taking care of me on these occasions – so much bigger, noisier and more exciting than anything in our usual quiet lives. Remarkably, George did just that. I always felt protected by George (at times even irritatingly over-protected), although I was the pushy one and he was shy.

Only once did George let me down, only once in all those childhood years. Later I came to see that he too had been trapped, and I suspect it was almost as painful for him as it was for me. We lived perhaps altogether too sheltered a life. Guests of my parents brought two sons with them, close in age to George, perhaps a year or so older. We were all sent out to play together in the back yard. The visiting boys' idea of play was to torment and humiliate the youngest child available. They soon discovered the 'pit' in the garage – the underground space used for servicing my father's car, a dark, oily space covered with heavy boards when not in use. They declared I would be too scared to climb into it. No problem; I had often been there, even with most of the boards down. They dared me to go and promised not to put the boards on, turning to George to confirm the promise ('We won't, will we, George?'). Too innocent to recognise a nod and a wink when he saw one, George agreed that they wouldn't. But of course they did, and tramped on them when I tried to push them up. I am absolutely clear to this day that I was still not afraid of being there but was completely broken up by the betrayal: the sense that I had been lied to, that no one there was on my side, that even my trusted brother stood by (what else could he do?). When they let me out I rushed sobbing uncontrollably to Nannie in the nursery, followed by mocking laughter.

Telling the truth was high on the list of virtues we were taught to strive for. I particularly remember lying as something my father took very seriously. On the whole I am grateful for the awareness of truth, and of its value, that my father's insistence ingrained in me. I certainly can't claim always to have been truthful, but deliberate lying has never come

easily or without troubling my conscience. I can even remember several of the few occasions on which I lied, usually to my mother, of whom I was afraid.

Children who lied were bad. But adults lied to us, and felt free to deceive us. Scrapes and cuts were common, and on one occasion I was – understandably – resisting the painful application of iodine by the trained nurse who was my father's secretary. George was present, and the nurse was inspired to say that it really didn't hurt, and she would demonstrate this by applying it to George. Of course it didn't hurt on unbroken skin, so I was the more offended when it was put on my cut, and the more convicted of unacceptable cowardice when I bellowed.

More seriously, I still remember being lured on some pretext or another into my father's surgery, usually a forbidden area. I was suddenly snatched up and held down, with a terrifying rubber mask held over my face. I was being anaesthetised with chloroform, fighting and kicking, for the removal of my tonsils. I am sure it was a privilege to have the specialist perform the operation in my own home, but young as I was at the time – perhaps four or five years old – I believe I would have managed much better had I been told what to expect. I had several such minor operations as a small child, and was never given any warning.

Then, when I was about nine, I contracted appendicitis, as my brothers had at the same age. It happened during our summer holiday, which inconvenient timing was also curiously part of the family pattern (my brothers had set the example in previous summers), but this time with the added complication that we were abroad. We were in Belgium, and my father could not bear to contemplate a foreign hospital, probably staffed by non-English-speaking nuns (anathema to his Protestant and rather xenophobic soul) and where, more importantly, he would not be in control of the standard of asepsis rightly so important to him. He thought my condition quite urgent – he had in fact made the diagnosis when I had a mild attack a few weeks previously, but had been labelled over-anxious by a colleague.

There was talk of flying home, a rare way to travel at the time, but the weather was bad, so after several days my parents and I took a ship, leaving Nannie to finish out the holiday with my two brothers. It was perfectly clear to me what was happening. I did not have the courage to ask a direct question – I wonder how it would have been answered? –

but I found myself waiting tensely for the adults to pounce, literally. When my father finally told me the diagnosis – an hour or so before the operation – and told me that he would hold my hand as I went under, my only feelings were of relief and gratitude that I had been told, not taken by surprise. I was praised on that occasion for my bravery. They should rather have been congratulated for finally coming to their senses.

My appendectomy was done at a nursing home in London, by a distinguished London surgeon. Harold was very well thought of by his London colleagues. Perhaps he acquired his reputation before he left the London Hospital; perhaps it derived from his war service. He was certainly still well known among the London medical fraternity. While I was in the nursing home, I had a continuous stream of visitors, mostly bearing gifts. It was common to be hospitalised for a fortnight after surgery; my stay was longer because I had an embolism, a blood clot, very rare in a child my age, but more common at that time because of the belief that bed rest was good. Now it is understood that movement after surgery is essential. I remember that day clearly. I passed blood in my urine in the morning. The nurse removed the bedpan without comment (for which she was praised) but I had seen it and knew something was amiss. My mother, I think, was out of town that day, but my father spent the whole day by my bedside. He read to me, we probably worked on a jigsaw puzzle, but he could not hide his anxiety. Not a word of my illness was spoken – again, what a mistake. I was sure my father thought I was going to die. I was equally sure that I was not, and did my best to reassure him (but how?). The only relief he had from his fear was when a children's story he was reading to me took a moral turn he disapproved of, seeming to give credit to magical intervention rather than to personal effort, which made him cross enough to take his mind off my illness for a few minutes. In the end, of course, all was well – the story resolved satisfactorily, and I recovered. An x-ray showed a lesion on one kidney but I had no further problems. We returned to Plymouth in good order, though it may have taken me a while to recover from being so spoilt.

Harold was a general surgeon, which meant exactly what it says. I remember only one specialised surgeon in Plymouth at the time; Cyril Prance was an ear, nose and throat specialist, taking out endless tonsils and adenoids. My father was one of several other surgeons who did whatever else came their way, appendices, cancer, all kinds of abdominal surgery, orthopaedic, gynaecological, even emergency brain surgery. Plastic surgery was scarcely invented until the terrible burns of the Second World War, but Harold would work hard to give an acceptable appearance and speech function to a child born with a cleft palate. People did not forget the kind of service he gave. Many years later, after our house was badly damaged in an air raid during the war, a policeman and his wife came and helped us clear it out, glad, they said, to show their appreciation for what Harold had done for their daughter.

When our phone rang at night, it might be a call from a general practitioner, perhaps as much as sixty miles away, telling of a patient with acute appendicitis or the victim of a serious farm accident or an obstetrical emergency. Few people had telephones: by the time the local

Derry's Clock before the war

22

doctor had been belatedly summoned and made his decision to call a surgeon the situation could be dire. Harold never asked whether it was a 'paying patient' or not. He got into his car and drove. The operation would be performed at the nearest cottage hospital, or on the kitchen table or on his folding operating table. Later, he would talk with the doctor, and learn, perhaps, that the patient's family was going through a bad time, in which case no fee, or a very small one, would be charged. It was understood, however, that when the doctor's better-off patients needed surgery, he (or, rarely, she) would refer them, too, to my father. In other words, the richer paid for the poorer, without any state intervention. In regions of varied occupations and a range of incomes, like the Devon and Cornwall in which we lived, this could work quite well – paternalistically, but with a measure of human understanding – particularly as far as the work of a man such as my father was concerned. He probably did more than his share of non-paying night emergencies, because his attitude (not shared by all the Plymouth surgeons) became known, but most of the general practitioners respected him in return, and played the game fairly. And he loved the country work; he was always a farm boy at heart; as we drove, he always had a comment on the state of the growing crops along the roadside. The same system of fees graded by ability to pay presumably prevailed with his urban patients, but was not obvious to me because it lacked the drama of the night calls.

When I was in my teens, A.J. Cronin wrote *The Citadel,* a best-selling novel about medical practice. I read it and became an instant convert to the need for a national health service. I reread it recently and was astonished to find that it does not in fact say much about a public service, going only as far as advocating cooperative practice, but showing up many of the abuses to which the private system was prone. Another book that much influenced me in my late teens was Margery Spring Rice's *Working-Class Wives,* which opened my eyes to the lack of medical attention affordable by poorer women. I came to recognise that what I had been familiar with was unworkable in cities with a dense population of people living around the poverty line. Our mixed rural and urban region was also less badly affected by the Depression than northern industrial areas, though I do recall the hard situation of some of our acquaintances, especially half-

pay, forcibly retired army officers with no hope of employment. And poverty was visible around us; the children of the poor went shoeless in streets near the back of our house.

With Harold's fee scale ranging from none to moderate, never excessive, he prospered, becoming able to pay private school fees for all of us and – when I was ten – to buy our dream house.

Once, much later, my father told me that he regretted not being closer to us when we were children. I don't remember how I answered, but I hope I was able to reassure him. He seldom visited the nursery, but he was very much a presence in our lives. I don't think we ate our evening meal with our parents, but we did all the others. Even at breakfast, he was usually willing to interact with us with respect and good humour. I recall one exception, when he was preoccupied and snapped at me for some childish foolishness. He immediately apologised, which aberrant behaviour on the part of a grown up so overwhelmed me that I burst into tears, making a great nuisance of myself and calling down deserved anger from all.

He was always busy, almost constantly on call, but whenever he was not out of town he was home for lunch and sometimes took a break again for afternoon tea at half past four. Lunch was the big meal of the day. Jo, my mother, was challenged to have 'the doctor's' meal kept hot but not too hot, as he would need to eat quickly and be off again. He was often late to lunch and in a hurry. Sometimes my parents were relaxed at meal times, and we were not excluded from the conversation, within bounds.

Harold's main work was at the hospital, but his office for consulting and minor surgery was at our home on Lockyer Street, built on to the back and overlooking the back yard where we played – an occasional inconvenience as we were admonished not to disturb him or his patients by being too noisy. Probably our afternoon walks usually took us away during consulting hours, as I know we most often played without restriction. And, at my father's insistence, we always wore old clothes in the back yard and were positively encouraged to get dirty – Nannie, who had to clean us up when play was over, and Mother, who liked to have presentable children if a visitor came by, were not so pleased.

From very early years, teatime in the drawing room was a special pleasure to me, and not only because of the obligatory thin brown Hovis bread and butter or the cake or chocolate biscuit which followed. If Father had the time, I would climb on his lap after tea. I have particular memories of his regularly sharing the new issue of *Punch* with me, looking at the cartoons together, having the jokes explained. A series ran called 'Simple Stories', which he read to me. Superficially, they were indeed simple, even if I missed the not-so-simple adult meaning. The main joy anyway was sitting on his lap being read to. Every issue had a political cartoon in it. These we passed over, and I soon learnt to recognise the cartoonist's style and to impress my father by saying 'Oh, that one is just political' as I turned the page.

We had some unexpected opportunities to spend time with Father, sometimes at short notice, when he swept us up out of the nursery to go with him on one of his drives into the countryside, to see a patient or to operate at Tavistock, or some other place. George and I became quite familiar with the garden at Tavistock Hospital and at several private nursing homes in the area. We were well-behaved children, especially George, who was in charge when we were on our own, and evidently we were trusted not to get into any serious scrapes.

Better still, some expeditions took us on the ferry across the river Tamar into Cornwall. My father hated any kind of ostentation and was embarrassed when the emergency required that he had to go to the front of the line-up at the ferry; I thought it rather splendid. The world was much smaller in those days, and he – and perhaps his car – was known to many of the people whom we met on our drives. If the tide was low and there was a significant bump to drive on to the ferry, a man would run to put a board under the wheel of 'the doctor's' car. Once or twice we were even stopped by the police as we passed through some village on the way home from, perhaps, Bude, so that he could be directed to go straight to an emergency in Tavistock, rather than going home and having to come back.

Harold's sporty cars were his one major extravagance, rationalised by his need for speed as he drove through South Devon and all over Cornwall. Many if not most of his cases were urgent. People were often slow to call the doctor, the doctor sometimes slow to call the surgeon. Appendicitis in those pre-antibiotic days yielded to nothing but the surgeon's knife, and there were of course accidents of all kinds. His car had to be swift, small and manoeuvrable enough to go down the tiny

The Pier before the war

lanes of the west country, but spacious enough to hold his folding operating table, a modern device he had bought after years of operations done on kitchen tables. But this was not the whole story of his cars; he loved them for themselves, and whenever he had any justification, he would buy something out of the ordinary.

Many years later, playing a word game with one of my daughters, my grandchildren and my brother, George had them helpless with laughter as he reeled off the names of makes of sports cars, Alvis, Railton, Invicta, Lanchester, all of which our father had owned, none of which the younger generation had ever heard of. My mother mostly disliked them, especially the Invicta. Like most of them, he bought it second-hand. It had something called a floating dashboard, which was supposed to remain steady as the car bounced, but in reality jiggled madly in front of you all the time. And the front seats were, supposedly, inflatable, but on the passenger's side you would find yourself sitting on the baseboard. By now, Jo fortunately had her own Morris Oxford, a good reliable family car in which she took us for picnics.

Harold's clientele came to include the poor, the professional, and the comfortable middle class. It did not include the very wealthy or the titled, who would patronise only the big names of London Harley Street specialists. Just once, this pattern was broken. Mount Edgcumbe is one of the two arms that embrace Plymouth Sound, the wide bay, gateway to

26

the Channel, which is overlooked by Plymouth
Hoe. The Earl and Countess of Mount Edgcumbe
came and went at their own volition, more or less
invisibly, not, as far as I know, paying much
attention to Plymouth and its affairs – more
power to them: who would want to be constantly
trotted out as local show pieces? But one night the
countess became ill. The local doctor was called,
and the diagnosis was appendicitis too acute for there to be any question
of travel to London. My father was summoned: no simple house call, this.
The small passenger ferry had to put on an emergency midnight service
to bring him across – to save the time of a long journey by road and car
ferry. My father confirmed the diagnosis, picked the countess up – he was
a short, strong man – and carried her downstairs (this has always seemed
to me one of the most romantic and improbable parts of the story) to be
driven to the ferry and ultimately to a good Plymouth nursing home. For
my father it was pretty routine. He would have done the same for
anyone.

Oddly enough, I was a major beneficiary of the episode. A few months
later, coincidentally (and ironically) when I myself was in a London
nursing home following my emergency appendectomy, a parcel arrived
from Carrington, a London jeweller, containing a fine seed pearl
necklace, with a card inscribed '*By Desire of the Right Honourable the Earl of
Mount Edgcumbe*'. My mother had trouble concealing her envy. My father
had doubtless refused to name any wishes for himself beyond his fee, and
had perhaps mentioned me in conversation (the more leisurely recovery
time of those days allowed for a real acquaintanceship between surgeon
and patient). Moreover, I believe no one would have been comfortable
with jewellery given to another man's wife. The little necklace has been
worn for many years, first by me, then by my daughter Mary, and now
by her niece, my granddaughter Siara. We were also given an open pass
to walk in the grounds of Mount Edgcumbe. Nannie and I took
advantage of this a couple of times, and on one visit were given tea by
the housekeeper. This, for me, added to the story-book aura surrounding
the whole episode, as she entertained us with a horror story of an
Edgcumbe ancestor accidentally buried alive and brought to life by a
putative thief trying to cut a ring from her finger.

My eldest brother, Douglas, was seldom part of our life, having been
sent off to boarding school at the age of eight, but there often was a third
child in our nursery. Next door but one was the vicarage of St. Andrew's

church, and the vicar's daughter Mary, the youngest of four girls, was just a year older than I – between George and me in age. Her sisters were several years older, and her mother was often ill with a heart condition. Mary and I were fast friends from as early as I can remember. The last time I saw her was a full eighty years later, when my brother George and I visited her together in Hampshire, where she lived with her husband, another friend from those early days. Sometimes I visited the vicarage. I remember teatimes in a room with shining hardwood floors and many fascinating objects brought back from missionary journeys overseas, from delicate china to brilliantly coloured shell collections, to solid unattractive china buddhas, to a tiger-skin rug on the floor. Sometimes there were interesting visitors there. I sat on the lap of a bishop with a long white beard, whom later I identified in my historical research as Lord William Cecil, Bishop of Exeter, noted during the First World War for his vicious hostility to the conscientious objectors in whom I had by then become interested.

CHAPTER 3

Nursery Years

Nursery life was mainly peaceful, circumscribed by routine, and enriched by two sources of love and security in the persons of Nannie and my brother George. When my little friend Mary was visiting, which was often, Nannie revealed one inadequacy; she had only two sides. This meant when she read to us, someone was not cuddled up next to her. The physical closeness to Nannie was surely important – so little was such closeness encouraged in that culture – and I remember it also as one of the joys of being bathed. George was an unusual and wonderful brother. Two and a half years older than me, he was my playmate, but also my great protector. I don't clearly remember how this manifested itself, but the remembered sensation is profound. He was shy: I was bold. He was good: I was bad. But he was on my side. I do not know how much we talked about such things – probably very little – but I knew he was there for me.

Most days we spent some time outdoors in the small back yard. Originally there had been a circular lawn, but my father had almost the whole thing cemented over to make a better ground for our tricycles and battered old pedal-car. There was a rough grassy slope down towards the basement kitchen windows, and we were allowed to dig around in that at will. It proved to have a remarkable clay soil which lent itself to supreme mud pies and even primitive pottery. Our play often included building with the various bits and pieces of wood and junk that lay around, seemingly always in good supply for us to make use of.

We were not allowed outside the yard, except to go to the local sweet shop to spend our weekly pennies. On one occasion – it must have been Nannie's day out or even her annual holiday – George

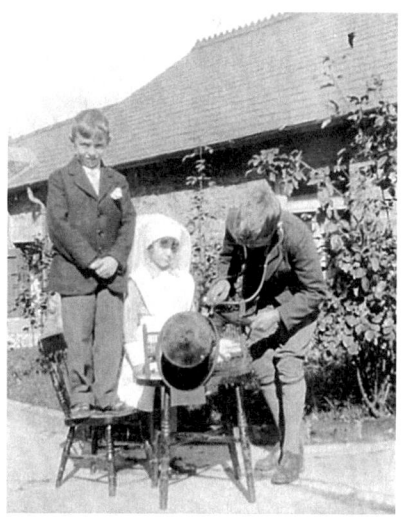

Two doctors and a nurse: George, Jo'phine and Douglas

29

and I decided to supplement our pocket money with an entrepreneurial venture. We gathered up some of our old weekly comics, mounted them on a board, and dressed ourselves in our most disreputable clothes – whether this was in the hope of exciting pity for our impoverished state or in the hope of avoiding recognition I can't remember. The enterprise was successful only in that no one ever found out about it. We had fixed

Playing at doctors and nurses

the price at one penny, probably half the new price, and stood outside the sweet shop, hopefully, for what seemed like a long time. One boy hesitated, and then said he only had a ha'penny. I was amazed and impressed when George immediately dropped the price to meet the resources of this potential customer. But the boy had the good sense to continue on his way into the sweet shop, where a ha'penny would buy a ha'p'orth of sweets done up in a screw of paper.

Another less-than-successful afternoon's play was the occasion when we acted out the Good Friday story. George made a wooden cross, on to which we nailed one of my cloth dolls, and we paraded around the back yard with the doll held high. To my parents' credit, we were not scolded, but we were told to stop, as some of the neighbours might find it offensive. The stigmata on the hands of my poor doll did not heal, and caused me some discomfort whenever I looked at her afterwards; fortunately she was not a favourite and was not often played with.

The nursery was equipped with a multi-volume *Children's Encyclopaedia,* and another set of something called *Arthur Mee's Book of Knowledge,* bought at one of the auctions and sales of furniture at old houses that were changing hands. My parents loved to go to these sales, and sometimes Harold managed to visit without Jo's moderating influence. He came home with a number of odd things, from an ancient dental chair – for which no use was ever found – to a number of superannuated sailor's life vests which, although not up to modern

30

standards, served us well and even travelled to Canada with my own young family many years later. But the encyclopaedias were a find. When they reached the nursery, both sets were in good condition, except for the first two volumes of the *Encyclopaedia.* Their covers were faded, patchy and blistered, and their pages were dimpled, with an uneven pink all round the edges, and a tendency to stick together.

Harold's love of a bargain had come up against his obsession with protecting us against germs, and he had tried to sterilise these unfortunate volumes in his surgical steam steriliser. He was almost a first-generation

Complex vehicles featured in many of our games. George, Jo'phine and Mary Daukes

descendant, in surgical terms, of the nineteenth-century discovery of the vital role of asepsis in surgical recovery and indeed of the crucial role of germs in disease. It would be close to another decade before the first antibiotics were developed. Children, especially, were prone to illness that came suddenly and in the face of which the doctor was often helpless. I am glad that my father did not decide to suppress the rest of the *Encyclopaedia,* nor to continue its drastic treatment after he had almost ruined the two experimental volumes. He told me once that it had been a struggle to avoid taking his fear of germs to extreme lengths. He said he had been helped by his acquaintance with a colleague who could not open a door without first wrapping a clean handkerchief around the handle. But he also liked to sing a song from his days as a medical student: 'Bertie, Bertie, you're so dirty/ You're rubbing your britches/ against those stitches/ Where do you think you'll go?'

It was rare for us to complain of boredom. We seldom ran out of ideas for imaginative play. At times, with Nannie's help, we dressed up, usually

31

In the backyard: George, Nannie, Doug (home from school), and Jo'phine

as stereotypical figures, George, the doctor in striped pants and top hat, me as nurse in an apron with a red cross on it. More to my taste, the navy featured large in our play, and when my mother allowed me to wear my reefer jacket (a navy blue garment complete with brass buttons) to play in, I was in seventh heaven. This increased my chance of sometimes being allowed to be the captain, not the lowly tar or the evil pirate. Or sometimes it was cowboys and Indians. And always after the Christmas season, we got several weeks of play out of our elaborations on whatever the Christmas pantomime story had been. Indoors, we were fortunate in the toys that we had, which lasted a long time. I particularly recall a very substantial set of construction bricks, from a German toymaker, which lent themselves to a variety of imaginative play. We did not think of them as ours, as they had been left for us by a family going overseas – who never came back to collect them. I had dolls and a teddy bear (also, I admit with embarrassment, a 'golliwog', a soft 'blackface' doll popular then), and George had a battered clown. I had a doll's pram, and a little china tea set. I had a dolls' house, rather an inadequate one made of an old packing-case – until my mother made one of her most brilliant contributions, which I will recount below. We played out and built on the stories we read and that were read to us. Alas, too many of them reflected the imperial era in which we were growing up, with its military, racist and colonialist colouring.

One memory from those nursery days appears to be somewhat unusual – as a memory, though it is of an experience that must surely be common to us all. I wish I knew what age I was at the time, quite young,

I think, perhaps no more than an infant. I was looking across the room at someone, perhaps Nannie, more probably my brother, and it dawned on me that this other person had their own sense of self, their own centre, a view and thoughts that were as real as mine but quite other. I remember feeling disoriented, almost dizzy, more than a little uncomfortable and scared; it was too big and consequential a thought to grasp. I pushed the revelation away within a few seconds, but returned to it from time to time during the next days, becoming more familiar with it, although not entirely comfortable. I wonder whether we ever do become completely at ease with the concept that every other person has a centre as complete and valid as our own, into which we can never enter.

A memory such as this reaffirms my disagreement with those philosophers, psychologists, whatever, who maintain that what makes us human is language and that there is no thought without words. I know that the profound realisation about the awareness of others came to me long before I had the words to express it. Even now I cannot quite capture it in words. And I also have a much vaguer, but I think accurate as far as it goes, recollection of finding, as my vocabulary grew, that words irritatingly slowed down my thinking. First, I would have a thought. Then, the words would try to catch up with it (that is, I would be compelled to try to put it into words), sometimes getting in the way of the next thoughts that were hurrying along ahead. I learnt to read very early, and that caused me, in addition, to see many of my thoughts in writing in my head. I remember the awkwardness of always having at least two streams of traffic in my head, moving along at different speeds and not always in exactly the same direction. For many years now, words have been to me a joy, a precious possession. I glowed recently when a friend called me a wordsmith. The benefits of reading were many, yet I still wonder whether such early reading inhibited something exciting and creative.

My father was always looking hopefully for mechanical ability in us, regardless of gender, and it was a disappointment to him when I rather quickly exhausted the possibilities of a clockwork train. I have still not figured out what more I could have done with the wretched little circular track on which it ran round and round. George's Hornby train had much more scope. Very occasionally, under careful adult supervision, the boys' small working steam engine was fired up. But most of our play was not gender-specific. George and I played together in all our games. Nannie made jigsaw puzzles with us, she made fudge and toffee on the nursery gas ring, she helped us with sundry paper and glue projects, she did

Messing about in water: a picnic

simple scientific experiments with us out of those remarkable encyclopaedias, she cuddled us and read stories to us, and she bathed us and wrapped us in big bath towels.

Nannie's life with us was a busy one. She had many daily chores, though I was scarcely aware of some of them. I am not even sure whether she did our laundry. She certainly did a lot of ironing and starching – her own uniform included starched cap, collar and cuffs. In the nursery, she was often busy sewing for us, and for my mother, working on a hand-driven Singer sewing machine, or stitching by hand. Curiously, she was responsible for making butter for us, another spin-off from Harold's efforts to keep us safe. Tuberculosis was rampant, spread by infected milk; pasteurisation was not yet compulsory. But some herds and their pasture were regularly tested and guaranteed tuberculosis free. All our milk and cream came from 'TT' herds, but TT butter was not available. So rich cream was bought, and it was Nannie's job to churn it into butter. We had some kind of device supposed to make this easier, but mostly Nannie spurned it as no help at all and did the work, as I recall, with a hand whisk, not too difficult when the cream was heavy enough, but a time-consuming chore when it was thinner. It did not come labelled with neat percentages in those days.

Nannie's butter-making led to my visiting the kitchen with her occasionally, a relatively rare opportunity. In our culture, girls were expected to grow up into housewives, albeit servant-employing housewives. I cannot fathom how we were to be equipped for this when we never even saw housework done, being kept from the kitchen, removed from the nursery when it was cleaned, were not in the room when the beds were made, and saw no laundry and little washing-up done. I did sometimes go shopping with my mother, particularly enjoying the market, where there were live as well as dead rabbits. I disliked the smell of blood in the butcher's shop, carpeted with clean sawdust, but I never connected it with the rare roast beef that I relished.

Perhaps the thinking was that children would learn these things later. I wasn't taught to make my own bed until just before I went to boarding school at the age of twelve. The adults of my childhood could not know what I am now convinced is so, that later instruction will never take the place of simple exposure from infancy. Small children are observant, they want to know how things are done, and they want to help. They just absorb what they are exposed to. The coming of the Second World War changed things mightily, and of course I learnt when I had to, and learnt much more when I got married. In the Women's Royal Naval Service (WRNS) I met some who felt the work required of us in basic training was beneath their dignity. I am glad to remember that my reaction was rather one of shame that I simply did not know how to set about scrubbing a floor, and was so inept at it. A general sense of inadequacy as a housewife stayed with me most of my life, although long ago I made a conscious decision not to let it bother me, and gradually, though practice did not make perfect, I managed.

And where was our mother all this time? Well, not as completely absent as I may have made it sound. Jo, my mother, had wanted so much to be married, and had, I am sure, felt fulfilled by her engagement to Harold, my father, one of the most highly regarded young surgeons of the time. Even as a senior nurse (a 'Sister' in charge of a ward or an emergency department), she had been subject to regimentation by the hospital matron. She told a story of her last obligatory Christmas dinner eaten at the matron's table. Christmas puddings customarily contained a selection of small charms, each one supposed to predict the future of the lucky or unlucky finder. In her portion, Jo found a button. The matron looked over her glasses and said, 'Oh dear, Sister, I fear that means that you will remain a spinster!' Jo, who had become engaged a few days previously, but was not yet ready to announce it, countered with, 'I am not so sure, Matron, it looks rather like a trouser button!', a retort that was

My mother dressed for riding

35

In the Folly at Mount Edgcumbe

received with severe disapproval – as borderline risqué.

I suppose part of what my mother wanted out of marriage was a respected life of relative leisure. I do not know whether she had hoped to work alongside her husband, doing at least part of the job done by his secretary-nurse, and I don't know why, by the time of my earliest memories, she never did this. I suspect it was some part of the hierarchical class system. It was all right for the wife of a general practitioner to assist her husband in this way, but it was not expected of a consultant's wife. Jo had been well educated in the excellent Scottish schools of her time. She had been fiercely independent as a young woman, insisting on carving out a career for herself. But she was not independent of social mores, and cared a lot for status. So – as I remember it – her routine day was to plan meals with the cook, perhaps meet her friends down town for morning coffee, and read endless novels. I am sure she was thoroughly bored.

Whatever the reason, I remember her as often bad-tempered, and as quite often clouting me unexpectedly, if perhaps not undeservedly. When George and I fought I probably was the one who started it, certainly this was assumed without the need for enquiry. I was prone to rage (did I take after my mother in this?), and it is no wonder that George showed up much better than I did. I came to think of myself as a very bad little person. I remember a distinct sense of relief later when I was chatting with schoolmates and found that several of them had bitten their brothers regularly and did not feel particularly bad about it. I am not sure how often I bit George; probably only a very few times. I do remember the sense of sin that followed such an episode. More than the punishments, I think I was hurt by the sense of not being loveable. I once overheard my mother, in conversation with a friend, comparing me to George, saying something to the effect that I was not only more troublesome, but that I was quite unfeeling when scolded, whereas

George was sensitive to the least indication of reproach. I think it quite wrong to imbue a child with such a sense of sin, or to assume that they are unfeeling, let alone to compound it all with the common error of believing that they do not understand what is said about them.

Yet there is a contrasting thread mixed into this tangled skein of memories. I was aware of my flaring rages as something I needed to get a grip on – I frightened myself – and I was glad to have help in gaining that control. I do not know who it was that gently persuaded me (it may have been Nannie) but at some level I welcomed learning that it was within my power to make that change.

The times when my mother was not unhappy and bad-tempered were the times when she had something of interest to do. It seems unlikely that a child under ten years old would be aware of this, but I recall it with conviction. Holidays were good. There were some special times when she and Harold went away together for a few days, perhaps even to London. And family summer vacations were important to her. When I became ill in Belgium, lying in bed in the hotel, I overheard her weeping in the next room, and complaining to Nannie. Although I could not hear the words, I believe her distress was more because it put an end to her annual summer holiday than out of anxiety for me and my developing appendicitis. She would have been happy to send Nannie back to England with me. It may have been one of the rare occasions when my father put his foot down. In retrospect, I can almost understand her distress at the unexpected end of her anticipated holiday. But I may have altogether misinterpreted her distress; in general she was at her gentlest when we were ill. I remember feeling safe and at ease in her presence whenever I was suffering some childhood complaint. Fortunately, I did not choose hypochondria as a route to her affection, perhaps because just as she nursed me with tenderness, it was she who also decreed when I was better.

Other than holidays, there were good times for my mother when something demanding came along to challenge her, to enable her to put her considerable organising skills to work, or just to provide a new experience. She worked hard at a major fund-raising drive for the Plymouth hospitals, lasting over several months and involving a number of events. My first and never-to-be-matched success on the stage was part of this. Children were recruited from all the doctors' and other professional families. We were coached by quite a gifted and certainly courageous young man into a performance of A.A. Milne's *Make Believe*, put on at a real little theatre, compete with curtain, wings and some kind of dressing-rooms. The work consists of three disparate acts, each a play in itself, linked only – loosely – by the prologue and epilogue. I played Jill, the major female part in the central act. Jill was a little girl much like myself, so there was little acting. I had no trouble speaking loudly enough to be heard, and learning the prodigious script was surprisingly not a big problem. Oddly enough (or so it seemed to me) the script mocked doctors, clergy and governesses, which added to my enjoyment. I do remember some anxious coaching by the governess, Nannie and my mother, but at the age of eight I found it easy to learn by heart. I wonder whether, in turning away from rote learning – indeed, despising it – as we have now

for many decades, we are not simply failing to take advantage of a useful gift that may occur at a certain stage of maturation. I do not remember other activities of the hospital fund-raising, except for a curious formal ceremony at which I gave a token purse to some princess or other who came to open something – the fair? a new hospital wing? But I remember my mother's animation and enjoyment.

Living in Plymouth, we had easy access to Dartmoor, still my favourite countryside. I think my father valued his country

Nannie on Dartmoor

upbringing so highly that he always felt guilty that we had to live in town; so he encouraged us to spend time on the moors. My mother made good use of her car to drive us out to beloved spots for picnics. Only years later, when she left directions for her ashes to be scattered on the moor, did I realise how deeply she and I shared a love of this wild country.

My eldest brother, Douglas, had a horse of his own, a mare named Watchful. George and I had riding lessons. After George went to school, my mother took me every week to Miss Cave Penny's riding school, way beyond Dartmeet. She was soon dissatisfied with the routine of sitting around waiting for me to return from an hour's ride and instruction, and, greatly daring, decided to take lessons herself. Jo had been well over forty when I was born, so at this time she was probably a little over fifty. Nowadays, most of us consider that as still young: then it was getting past middle age. She decided my father would not approve of the risks involved, so she did not tell him, swore those of us who knew to secrecy, and valiantly concealed the inevitable muscular stiffness which followed the early lessons. She bought herself a dashing and fashionable dark chocolate brown riding outfit, and thereafter, the riding lessons were focused on her, not on me. I suppose Miss Cave Penny was (perhaps sensibly) scared of the consequences should this elderly maverick suffer an injury when her husband had not even known she was riding. I have no idea how long the secret was kept. But I do remember her pleasure, although I somewhat resented what was virtually the end to my own learning of new skills – and we never galloped any more.

The episode also, indirectly, sheds light on Harold's generosity and wisdom, both perhaps remarkable for their time. I was told later, by my brother, that my father thought Jo prone to extravagance. He dealt with this not by monitoring her spending and questioning every purchase, but by giving her her own car and the most generous allowance he could afford, and – apparently – establishing a mutual understanding that she would stay within it but, otherwise, could spend it on whatever she wished.

I was the major benefactor of another of my mother's enterprises. Mother always put a lot of effort and imagination into Christmas. I feel a little sad at the extent to which surprise trumped shared anticipation and participation in her preparations. We never had any role in decorating the tree or wrapping parcels but were always presented with the fait accompli on Christmas morning. But at least the surprise was always positive, and her delight in our pleasure was manifest. One Christmas, when I was about eight years old, stands out. That year, instead of going to the drawing room for the tree and gift-giving, the event was held in our own nursery. There were a number of gifts piled up, including the usual brown paper parcels from those of the several aunts who sent family gifts every year, and even a few who packed up separate little gifts for each of us within a big packet. During the unwrapping of all these we scarcely noticed a large object behind the tree, rendered shapeless by being covered by a sheet.

At the end of the unwrapping, my mother told me there was one more gift for me. She turned on a switch and the five front windows of a big old Victorian dolls' house shone out through the sheet. My parents had found this amazing mansion several months earlier at one of those house sales they enjoyed, and had kept it hidden in the basement. This was the early 1930s, when anything of the Victorian era was held in little regard, and had yet to attract either interest, or value as antique – and there was

My doll's house was almost exactly like this one, which is in a museum in Canada

the usual caveat about possible germs. My mother had done a splendid renovation job on it, repainting it inside and out, refitting the kitchen, even fitting it with electric light by carefully running a set of Christmas lights around the rooms. Much of the original furniture had been put back in the up-to-date house – including, as I remember, a tallboy with a breakfront desk, a study desk just like my father's, a dining table and chairs, a four-poster bed, a washstand with a marble top, to which my mother later added a perfect miniature china washstand set (brought back from France), consisting of a jug, basin, toothbrush holder and soap dish, all decorated with tiny rosebuds. I sometimes watch the Antiques Road Show, and wish I had any one of these one-of-a-kind handcrafted pieces to bring for evaluation. But I still warmly appreciate the way in which it had all been completed with modern pieces, and was open and ready to play with. The scale was larger than what has now become the standard. The house, four rooms and a hall and staircase, took up a bit of space, but it was a good size to play with and could comfortably accommodate two of us children side-by-side in front of it.

A mostly new family was living there. Later I found two dusty Victorian children in our basement and was allowed to bring them up to join the family in what had been their old home. George and I both played endlessly with the house. He loved to make things work and fitted the fireplaces out with battery-lit fires that not only glowed but could be persuaded to flicker by loosening the bulb. The flat roof, behind a pediment, had been covered with green baize, and – again with the help of my mother – became a roof garden. From time to time we added other pieces. I remember finding some tiny pottery bowls and vases that I was able to fill with real flowers, the tiniest blooms I could find.

I loved this wonderful miniature house. I am sure that in more settled times it would have been one of the things that I would have managed to take with me as my life moved on, to be enjoyed by my children and even my children's children, entering a more and more respectable old age as a rare antique. When our house was damaged by bombing in the war, I passed it to a lovely family who were helping us take our things out of the house, and who had a child young enough to enjoy it for a couple of years. After the war, Nannie and I sought them out to take the house back. We were both sure that it had gone only as a loan. It turned out that their memory was different. When their daughter had grown out of it, they had in all good faith donated it to an orphanage. Nannie and I backed off at once, knowing how upset they would be if they realised that I still wanted it. I had to comfort myself with the thought that its size made it indeed a good toy for shared play. To this day, I sometimes think of the ironic fate of those unrecognised antique pieces of furniture, let alone of the house as a whole. I hope it was enjoyed for many years by children more deserving than myself.

CHAPTER 4

Governesses

In early middle age, particularly after we came to Canada, I gave up talking (except to my children) about my childhood. In retrospect it seemed to have been such a peculiar childhood, and also embarrassingly Victorian, which I thought might make people think me even older than I was. Even now, I feel compelled to point out that Queen Victoria had been dead for a good many years when I was born, and Jo, my mother, was no Victorian. Having had an English-style nannie is not what gave my early life that nineteenth-century flavour, odd though that may sound to Canadian ears. In the twenties and thirties quite a lot of English children had nannies. It was the governesses, and that more by their nature than by the mere fact of their existence. My governess walked straight out of Victorian fiction.

In accordance with the law, when George was five his formal education had to be seen to begin, and he began to attend a class every morning at the vicarage next-door-but-one, under the tutelage of a gentle soul called Miss Gover. I missed him painfully, and was probably a great nuisance without him, so within a few weeks my parents sent me to join him and my friend Mary, the vicar's daughter, a fine arrangement for me, but probably not the best for George.

In order, I assume, to keep the cost down, and presumably filling a perceived need, as many as ten or twelve children were enrolled at this time. I have no idea what the age range was – all the others seemed very big to me, but not intimidating, since they took no notice of me. For the gentle Miss Gover, however, we were a handful. Her problem was compounded by the chronic illness of Mary's gentle but largely invisible mother, who had a heart condition not then treatable, which would in fact lead to her death when Mary was ten years old. Meanwhile, and at some times more than at others, Miss Gover seems to have been abjured to keep us quiet. Impossible: we were totally disorderly. I do not think there was much if any fighting, we were just noisy, noisy, noisy. From time to time, even more desperate than usual to achieve a moment's relief, Miss Gover held a pin up high, declaiming that she wanted to know whether we could be so quiet that we would actually hear a pin drop. She got what she wanted, instant, total, blessed hush. But she could not hold the pin up indefinitely, and when she dropped it, we all cried out loudly and competitively, 'I heard it! I heard it!'

I expect there were some organised lessons, even resulting in periods of relative quiet. I was outside both the mob scene and the lessons. Considered too young for the latter, I spent most of my time on the floor under the table. One of the things Miss Gover tried to fill my time with was as pointless an occupation as I have ever encountered, a curious exercise (in self-discipline? in hand control? in frustration?). We had small individual black cardboard chalk boards (not slates), and she would make a dot in the middle of mine and tell me to go round and round it with the chalk, leaving no black spaces, until the whole board was full. I am prepared now to swear that this is impossible in practice, however doable in theory: I went on trying, and failing.

Not all my time was wasted, by any means. While I was under the table, usually by myself, the older children were probably sitting around the table doing something more formal in the way of lessons. With me under the table was a set of wooden letters of the alphabet, which I would contentedly arrange into alphabetical order. Somehow I feel sure that it was Nannie who had told me that learning the alphabet was the key to what I wanted to do most in all the world – to learn to read. I loved those dull, unpainted wooden letters. Miss Gover (or maybe it was Nannie at home?) must have taken the time and trouble to teach me the names and sequence of the alphabet. My understanding was, correctly, that the names of the letters were an essential tool in reading, and, less correctly, as I now see, that the order was equally important. For me, the last holdout was H, which would insist on getting in front of G.

So now with the order mastered, I could read. Back I went to Nannie with this precious knowledge, which she soon helped me turn into reality. She patiently allowed me to spell word after word out to her ('Nannie, what does C-A-T spell?', 'Nannie, what does S-A-T spell?', 'O-N?', 'T-H-E?' 'M-A-T?'). This began, as I clearly remember, first thing in the morning while she was trying to clean her teeth in the washbasin in the room I shared with her, and went on at intervals throughout the rest of the day – except, of course, for the few hours of compulsory schooling at the vicarage. Motivated as I was, and as one may well suppose Nannie also to have been, this intolerable stage was soon over, and I could indeed read simple books by the time I was three. Some children's books used to break the words up by hyphens between the syllables, and I found this very helpful – though soon I despised this crutch.

Later, I became interested in how children learn to read. In the everlasting controversy between phonics and sight-reading, I have always leaned to the side of phonics. I concluded that for most children, sounding out the letters, or spelling out the words, and indeed, even the repetitions and limited vocabulary of the sight method, all in fact morph into a glorified kind of phonics, as the symbols connect with sounds already known. For lucky ones like myself, an intense visual and perhaps emotional perception follows, which overcomes inconsistencies of English spelling and makes a word once read a lifetime possession. In any event, it all worked well for me, and I could read almost anything by the time I was four.

My education was going a great deal better than was George's. In accordance with the cruel practice of the time and culture, George was to

be sent off to boarding school at about eight years old. However, when the time drew near, our parents suddenly woke up to the fact that George could not read, and, thank god, they were not heartless enough to send him off so lacking. I do not think he could have benefited as I did from the under-the-table education that served me so well. Later in life he and I both realised that he had been quite severely dyslexic. I visited him once with my eleven-year-old dyslexic grandson, his great-nephew (whom I was teaching to read at the time), and he was moved by what he recognised of his own childhood disability, traces of which never left him. Late in life, when he became interested in writing about some of his experiences, he would occasionally email me to clarify the spelling or meaning of a word.

I am not sure where our parents' heads had been during the couple of years that we spent with Miss Gover. Nannie could have told them – or they could have observed – that when the weekly comic arrived, we spread it out on the floor between us, and I read it to George, to the satisfaction of us both. But the discovery that he could not read evidently was a shock, and Miss Gover was shortly dismissed. My friend Mary, the vicar's daughter, felt that the warm and likeable Miss Gover had been harshly and unfairly treated. She still recalled it that way when we last met, almost eighty years later, and she may have had a point. The situation was stacked against Miss Gover in a number of ways.

The pool from which governesses were drawn was part of the uncomfortable social fabric of the time, a component of the class system and of gender discrimination. Both Miss Gover and her successor were daughters of clergymen, impoverished in life, who had made a bad situation worse by fathering daughters and then dying young. The daughters had no training for anything, though some had quite a good informal education. What they had was a strong sense of social position, of what was proper for a 'lady', and of the need to hang on to their class status at whatever cost. Seeking a position as a governess or as a 'companion' were almost the only options. Jane Austen, Charlotte Bronte, Elizabeth Gaskell, writing in the previous century, would have recognised them. By the 1920s the situation was dire for those still clinging to the profession. Fewer people hired full-time tutors or governesses for their children, and for a shorter time. Our governesses were some of the last of the final generation. By that time most of us more fortunate girls went to private boarding schools, others to day schools, and those same schools often offered scholarships (though not always free of stigma) to clergy daughters.

My mother took an interest in Mary's welfare as well as in our education; the vicar's mind was often on higher things, and on his delicate wife, and Mary's three elder sisters seemed remote, but were probably struggling to keep the household afloat. Once Miss Gover's inadequacies were revealed, Jo played a leading role in her replacement, and it was agreed that our nursery would be the new classroom. She advertised the post, and interviewed applicants, or perhaps the only applicant; I saw only the one. I was called down to the drawing room to meet with Miss Straw. My mother handed me the novel she was reading, and the newspaper; I read fluently from both of them. Miss Straw expressed restrained approbation, but later, after she had secured the job, she told me nastily that she had not thought I read at all well. 'You read much too fast', she said. Unfortunately she made no distinction between the art of reading to oneself and the craft of reading aloud, and her determined efforts to slow me down at both were, alas, lamentably successful. I never became the super-speedy reader that I think I had the potential to be, at the age of six.

When Miss Straw came to us, she was already elderly. Her cheeks were rouged and powdered with a peculiar makeup that was applied via a thin paper tissue. She wore old-fashioned clothes, and round her neck was a piece of netting, edged with wire encased in black velvet; I was told this might have something to do with a thyroid condition. All this elicited some awe from me, but certainly not as much sympathy as the governess deserved. She was desperate not to appear too old for the job.

Miss Straw brought quite a new dimension to the nursery. Our regular class now consisted only of George, Mary and myself, although occasionally one or two others would be added temporarily. All of us ate lunch together in the dining room with my parents, and the only reason I remember one pair of sisters, named Biddy and Tishy, is that they always seemed to have heavy colds. My father (in their absence) always referred to them as Sniffy and Sneezy. Although he said this jokingly, he really did rather dislike them, seeing them as a constant source of childhood infections. They were not with us long. Others, mostly the children of transient naval or military families, also made only brief stays with us.

For three or four hours every morning (surely with a break for elevenses), the nursery became a classroom. We sat around the big old wooden table and worked hard at reading, writing, and arithmetic. Miss Straw presided with a light ruler with which she might occasionally tap us across the knuckles for inattention or some other delinquency. She seldom used it. The morning began with the recitation of a motto, chosen by the favoured pupil of the day from a very limited selection. I can still remember some: 'Habit is a cable, every day in every way, we weave a strand'; 'If at first you don't succeed, try, try again'; 'Pride goes before a fall', 'Good, better, best, I will never rest, Until my good is better, and my better best.' I hated them all.

Four hours a day, five days a week, was considered ample time for young children to give to formal education. I do not know how common this was in that day, but it was a matter of principle with Harold, my father, that young creatures should never be worked too hard (he used young horses as an analogy), and apparently our hours were enough to satisfy the authorities. Looking around me in the twenty-first century, I

46

am sure that we have come far too far from this precept. We had time for indoor and outdoor play, most of it depending on our own imaginations. We had plenty of time for exercise. The afternoons continued to be given to walks, although at an earlier period we had – briefly – attended a gym class with an army drill sergeant, and even more briefly, a swimming class with a navy instructor: at both I had been the youngest and one of the few female participants, and as such had been treated with uncharacteristic kindness by the instructors. George had been less fortunate and I think we quit the swimming class because Nannie had reported that the instructor's idea of how to teach a small boy to swim was to throw him in at the deep end. George had nearly drowned.

Regrettably, Miss Straw had persuaded my parents that she should be with us for the afternoon as well as the morning; even this was a reluctant comedown from the full-time resident position that she would have thought proper. But now, this meant the varied walks with our young Nannie were replaced by dull ones with Miss Straw, usually consisting of a perambulation on Plymouth Hoe – which beautiful and interesting place I came to consider boring in the extreme – and a rest, when it was not too cold, on a bench, while our governess read to us and I infuriated her by reading ahead, silently but obviously. I don't think I did it to annoy; I couldn't help it.

Lessons were not fun, but I loved to learn. Miss Straw had a good command of the limited subject matter, and was a competent teacher. I found out when I went to school that I was ahead of my contemporaries in arithmetic, but I knew every kind of exercise by an out-of-date name. She taught penmanship, and more importantly, she taught such tools as punctuation, and taught them thoroughly. I think she even encouraged some creative writing. It was in part my own fault that what came from me was clichéd and sought approval from the grown-ups rather than coming from any deep place in myself. But by the time I was nine, a writer was definitely one of the things I was going to be.

Miss Straw also claimed to be able to teach piano. For a short time previously we had had lessons from another visiting teacher. She had not been particularly good at the job. Miss Straw was worse, and I had no gift for it. I never even realised that, generally speaking, the top line carried the tune, so that it was years later that I discovered the ease and the real pleasure of picking out a recognisable tune. In order to keep us both occupied at the same time, Mary and I were set to play duets. Although Mary was considerably better than I, the result was a mish-mash of stumbling and unintelligible sound, with no recognisable tune or shape to it.

The tragedy of Miss Straw's situation was exacerbated by the fact that her two younger sisters had swallowed their pride and entered into state school teaching, lowering their social class but ensuring them employment, and a pension on retirement. She wore the snobbery for which she had made such sacrifices like a badge. Indeed, she went on and on about the importance of class, constantly commenting that she 'knew whether a person was a lady before she even opened her mouth' (accent being of course one of the acknowledged criteria). It was understood that my mother was a lady (despite her Scottish accent), Mary's mother was a real lady, Nannie of course was not, even less so the maids. Whoever else swam into our limited vision or formed part of an anecdote was assigned to one side or the other of the ledger. Female behaviour was classified as ladylike, unladylike or, if completely outside the pale, as 'common'. A great deal of this was framed within what Miss Straw saw as her difficult task of seeing to it that my behaviour became more ladylike. I am glad to say that, important as she made it out to be, I was as unimpressed as she was unsuccessful. I bless my family for their fairly easy acceptance of my identity as a tomboy; indeed, my father encouraged it, although I think my mother would have loved to have a prettier and more dressable little girl. I bless Nannie too, and have been struggling to define what was her role in countering the aura of snobbery that entered the nursery with Miss Straw. We did speak of the governess in her absence, we laughed gently together at her foibles. Nannie, I believe, with characteristic wisdom and generosity, managed to allow and even join in some gentle mockery of her artifices, without ever encouraging disrespect for her role or her competence as a teacher. She was always friendly and genuinely kind to Miss Straw.

We never felt close to poor Miss Straw, and perhaps waged an underground rebellion in some small respects. George and I discovered, for instance, that the inkwells could be satisfyingly sabotaged by injecting a mere drop of Nannie's sewing-machine oil, and, being spillproof, could not be emptied out to clean. A small, rather mean rebellion. On the whole, we behaved well, and learnt what we had to.

After a couple of years, George was able to read well enough that he could be sent off to school. Our parents drove him off to a private 'prep' school, located in a big old house standing in beautiful grounds near Tiverton, some two or three hours distant. When it was time to leave, he was summoned from the nursery for the obligatory serious short talk from our father (which, I learnt much later from George, had left him completely mystified; Harold's medical education had apparently done nothing to rid him of the view that sex was not a fit subject for family discussion) and to be given his pocket money, ten shillings for the term. Even then I think both George and I had a sense of the depth of the separation that was taking place. I was moved but no less bereft when George came back upstairs to give me one of his precious shillings before being whisked away.

There would never again be the same openness between us that we had shared in those early days. The boarding-school world of boys was in large part nasty and brutish, and few boys talked of its true nature when they were home for the holidays, though they would share stories of approved activities, especially sports. I suspect that George's generation had some particularly bad experiences with the leavening of masters who had entered teaching straight from the battlefields of the First World War. Even in the twenty-first century, the lasting effects of post-traumatic stress are not always acknowledged. At that time, shell shock, as it was called, was something to be ashamed of and denied by those who suffered from it. Not until some six or seven decades later would I be privy to some part of what George endured both at the prep school and at his public school.

CHAPTER 5

Mount View:
Getting the Country into the Child

When George went off to boarding school, the holidays became the highlights of my life. Briefly, our parents contemplated sending me off to join George at school. The headmaster and his wife had a daughter of my age, who went to the school for classes, but lived privately with her parents, who now sought a companion for her. I went to stay at their home for a week or two, but for whatever reason, the plan was dropped. I am sure my presence would not have been a good thing for George, and I doubt that I would have benefited either. Although perhaps I might have got a better start in Latin, then always a must for educational advancement, and always to be my Achilles heel. Who knows? I might also have become a cricketer. I remember the daughters of boys' prep school masters as shining lights at this sport.

George's social circle was now wider than mine and included the sons of the other leading Plymouth surgeon, Kennedy. All four of the sons went to the same school as George. They were known as Major, Minor, Tertius and Quartius – or could this youngest have been Minimus? I knew him as Peter. Although their home was on the same street as ours, I never came to know any of them well, except, briefly, Peter. He played opposite me in the remarkable production of *Make Believe*, which took place at about this time. Working with one of the Kennedy boys, George edited a 'magazine' called the *Black Cat*, all handwritten, which we proudly inflicted on our parents and their friends, charging a penny a read (but usually getting a little more). The proceeds went to the hospital fund-raising drive. I contributed a short story.

At home, big changes were on the way. My parents were house-hunting. Despite the Depression, Harold was prospering, and knew he could afford a house closer to meeting his dreams and those of his wife.

Had my father known I never noticed the changing seasons at that time, although I was now nearly ten years old, he would have felt his search to be urgent. It wasn't that we didn't spend time outside – come rain or shine, we were always outdoors for a large part of the day, playing in the back yard, walking with Nannie or our governess on Plymouth Hoe, even driving out with my mother for a picnic on Dartmoor. So why did the seasons mean so little to me? One reason was that, as children, our lives were totally under adult control: the grown-ups ordered our comings and goings, what we wore, what we ate. Although we might be at the nursery window reciting 'Rain, rain, go away, come again another day', we were inclined to put the blame on the adults for the postponed picnic. More importantly, we were essentially urban-based. The flowers in the flowerbeds on the Hoe must have reflected the seasons, but they were clearly as much the product of adult decree as were our clothes. Urban flowers bloomed in neat rows because they had been planted just so. But I do remember with joy special trips to pick wild daffodils or primroses in their seasons.

The house my parents found deserves to be remembered – by me of course, because it meant so much in my life, but also, in some strange way, for itself. The name of the house was Mount View. I do not know when it was given that name, now not uncommon and not particularly evocative. But in this case, the house had an absolute claim to the name. Standing on what was (at that time) the highest point within the Plymouth boundary, the house looked out between trees across land which dropped sharply away, and over the grounds of a small private boys' school and beyond that, over the trees and roofs of Plymouth to the sea, three miles away, to a different view of Mount Edgcumbe, Mount Batten and the three lighthouses familiar to me from my childhood walks on the Hoe.

We never knew the full history of Mount View. I wish I had had the

Mount View

51

View from my window at Mount View

interest and the background knowledge to do some research while we still lived there. Because of its elevation and outlook, the site had been actively engaged in the seventeenth-century Civil War: this much we knew because old cannon balls were found in the cellars, and it was later confirmed that a long, winding stone-walled passage down there had been built as a fortification. Whether any dwelling stood on any part of the site at that time I do not know. Usable cellar space was limited to two or three small storage areas. Gaps in the stone cellar walls led into areas full of rubble from some long-demolished building, whose walls did not coincide with the walls of the existing house. Between the rubble and the underside of the ground floor there was a scant crawl space, with which my father had gained some familiarity in the process of having the plumbing and electricity of the house brought up to date. From all this we deduced that there had been a substantial building before the one that we knew, despite the fact that Graham Naylor, a Plymouth historian who recently has generously answered a number of my questions assures me that no earlier building can be found at that location on any of several reputable maps.

I wish I had asked my father what he knew of Mount View's history from the deeds of the house. The front, facing out to the sea, had a Victorian-looking façade and undoubtedly much had been added and modernised in the late nineteenth century. But the layout of the house was more that of a perfect smallish version of an eighteenth-century classical house, often called Georgian. Much, much later, a Canadian professor of eighteenth-century history described the layout and proportions of well-known North American residences of that era. When he turned to me and asked if I had seen similar houses in the UK, I was startled into blurting out that I had grown up in one. (I hope I said a small version of one.) Even then it probably sounded boastful, pretentious, but as he talked, the high ceilings, the big windows, the lovely proportions and general liveability of Mount View had come back to me in a rush of homesickness. I may be imagining its earlier genesis, but no one can conclusively prove me right or wrong: Mount View was pulled down in the 1980s. And although evidence seems to suggest that it was built in the 1850s, I have no reason to distrust my recollections of the house we loved and lived in for those few years.

We were all full of a sense of excitement about the purchase. My parents found the house, fell in love with it, made their plans and put in a bid on the day it was auctioned. I remember going for a walk with Nannie that day, knowing that by tea time we would know whether the house was to be ours. We came back to find that we had been successful – I think the price was £6,000 but it may have been £4,000. Apparently, even then, this was a good price (these were, after all, Depression times). In any event it enabled Harold to set aside ample money for renovations.

My mother described the house to me, and particularly told me how I would love the garden, but I saw very little of it until after the purchase. Both parents threw themselves into the planning and supervision of the renovations. My mother joked that Harold woke her up in the middle of the night when he finally solved the problem of finding the right space to build in a large walk-in heated linen closet. I remember feeling that I was being kept out of the way altogether during this exciting time. But now, when I sit down to describe the house, I realise that my memory includes such a vivid picture of how it had been before the renovations that I must have been taken there at least once or twice before the move. But even at moving time I had no hand in packing or unpacking, not even the packing of my own clothes and toys. I was sent to stay with friends to get me out of the way until the house was quite ready.

Mount View was a big house, much bigger than I have ever lived in since. Downstairs had a large dining room and drawing room, and also a breakfast room, which was big enough to use for all meals except when there were a number of visitors. My father had a hatch driven through from this room directly into the kitchen, for convenience of service. Even this inside wall was over two feet thick.

The kitchen premises were extensive. The large kitchen had a cool sunken larder leading off it. Leading off the kitchen passage were a large scullery, a pantry and a big room converted by my father into his carpentry workshop. Towards the back door there was a washroom for the convenience both of outdoor workers and kitchen staff. In this same area was another door, kept locked, behind which a steep flight of stairs led to an altogether separate cellar, a spooky place with a trapdoor covering an ancient deep, echoing well.

A round glass conservatory lead off the drawing room, and beyond that was a separate full-size billiard room. This was a joy to me as well as to my father, who had taken to billiards as a medical student and had taught me to play while I was still too small to see over the table without a stool to stand on. In Lockyer Street he had shared his private office space with a three-quarter size table. Off the hall my father had installed yet another loo, a 'gentleman's lavatory' for the use of family and visitors.

Jo in the conservatory at Mount View

54

By the front door was a small wood-panelled room – the only area in the house to be dignified with wood panelling. Above the panelling, set on to the plastered wall, were two or three sculpted cherubim. I believe this tiny room must have been converted into a mini-chapel by the religious nineteenth-century owners.

Upstairs there were six bedrooms and a room lined with bookcases that now took the place of the old nursery, as children's room and Nannie's sewing room, though appropriately enough dignified by the name of library. Nannie and I had, for the first time, separate bedrooms. My parents had, for the first time, separate bedrooms. My room had a view of the garden. Nannie's looked out along the side of the house to a glimpse of the sea, which was the major feature of the view from my mother's room and the spare bedroom. My brothers shared a room, in which was duly installed the gymnastic trapeze which had hung in their Lockyer Street room. Two more large bedrooms, for servants, were partway down the back stairs, in a part of the house clearly built at a different time, where the ceilings were lower and the windows smaller.

All the bedrooms had hot and cold running water – an up-to-date

Harold at Mount View

Four o'clock drawing room teatime at Mount View

convenience in the thirties – and there were two large bathrooms with great big British baths. Before Harold brought the bathrooms into the nineteen-thirties, these baths had been what I am sure was avant-garde in the late nineteenth century. The baths had been encased in solid mahogany panels, as had a shower, strongly resembling a sentry box sitting at the end of one of the baths.

Except for the servants' bedrooms on the back stairs, and the kitchen area, all these rooms, down and up, were arranged around a square, the hallway, not very large in itself, that extended right up through the house to a skylight in the roof . The staircase went up on three sides of the hall and led to a sort of open gallery or passage, lit by the skylight and banistered on the side looking down into the hall, with the other side formed by the walls and doors of all the bedrooms.

We knew in outline the story of the house from the mid-nineteenth century on, when it had been acquired – or built – by a prosperous local family, the Rookers. Alfred Rooker was Mayor of Plymouth from 1850–51 and again from 1873–74, by which time he and his wife were living at Mount View. The son of an Independent Minister in Tavistock, he practised law in Plymouth from the 1830s, and was well known and very prosperous by the time he acquired Mount View. The house was lavishly decorated, or redecorated – with as much love and sense of contemporary enthusiasm as Jo, my mother, now put into it – and the four acres of grounds were landscaped and planted by experts called down to Devon from the famous Kew Gardens.

Alfred Rooker and his wife had three daughters, one of whom died in infancy. A devout Christian and supporter of Sherwell Church, he travelled to the places of the Bible in 1875, and died in Beirut of an illness contracted there. His wife died in 1887 and the elder daughter in 1890. The younger daughter, Marian Rooker, born in 1852 and apparently the last of the family, lived out a solitary old age and died, in 1931, all in the low-ceilinged back room my father now took for his workshop. She had been attended by an elderly couple and latterly never as much as visited other parts of the house, or saw the view. Even the driveway outside her window was deliberately obscured by thick, high laurel bushes. She had had a pulley system installed in this dismal room, by which she could raise herself in bed and – presumably with some help – could even manoeuvre herself into the bath tub, also installed in her room. She had, as far as we knew, never left the house for many years. In our imaginations she became little more than a figure of fun, the terror of the small boys of the adjacent prep school, subsisting entirely on Dundee Cake – we found Dundee Cake tins here, there and everywhere around the house and in all the outbuildings, mostly empty, some occupied by screws, short pieces of string, nuts, bolts, washers, nails, broken pencils, all the miscellaneous items that inevitably gravitate to empty containers. The garden, much too large for one person to manage, was maintained by a single elderly gardener. No one else set foot in it.

An excerpt from the Church history, recently supplied by Graham Naylor, has added detail that does not change this history, but has made Marian more real to me, and touched me by the tragedy of her life. She is described in the history of Sherwell Church as an active and generous member, but there is no evidence of recent contact, or of friendships maintained as she aged. And, as a feminist, I was startled and moved to read that 'in her youth Miss Rooker intended to be a medical practitioner, but an accident prevented her from achieving her ambition. For hobbies she dabbled in mathematics and Greek.'

Some of Jo's friends exclaimed at the rich, thick Victorian wallpaper, carpets and hangings – the drawing room was papered in gold and a dark Prussian blue, the dining room in dark red and gold – and told her that she must keep it. Given the probable date of the Rookers' renovations, and what I recall of the paper I saw, I think what my mother tore out may have been a museum of William Morris decoration. But she did not want to live in a museum, nor were Victorian artefacts back in style then. Reluctantly, I have to come down on her side. She was right to replace every last bit with modern 1930s paper, paint and carpeting – not necessarily to my taste, then or now – but, rightly, to hers. She kept some of the beautiful heavy damask curtains, the Venetian blinds and the wooden shutters. As it happened, the last two would prove useful in the Second World War.

My mother took pleasure in the furnishing of my small bedroom, buying a suite of two small chests and a wardrobe – built-in cupboards were hardly to be expected at that time. Nannie was not consulted and disliked the furniture because the wardrobe was too narrow for coat hangers to go in sideways, and she also found the drawers in the chests too small. The bed was a narrow divan, probably exactly what I would have chosen, and for which Nannie made a fitted bedspread, suitable for a bed-sitting-room, an appropriate place to take visiting (girl) friends. Curiously, although the bedspread died an honourable death many years ago, I still until recently had the very ordinary bed, tucked into my study, and provided with a new mattress, awaiting the occasional guest and meanwhile collecting a clutter of papers. All my children slept in it at one time or another. It did not travel to South Africa, but when we came to Canada, we collected it from my parent's house and brought it along. That move was paid for by the Royal Canadian Air Force.

My room also had a good, small armchair with a high back, a gas fire, and before very long, a bookcase – the first major purchase I ever bought with my own carefully saved pocket money, supplemented by small gifts from visiting uncles. This, too, I still have. A great joy was a small antique desk (correctly called a davenport, I believe), which my mother had bought for me at the sale of contents of the house. I see it weekly when I visit my daughter.

Much of our furniture came with us from Lockyer Street. Nannie, who was as skilled at this as at dressmaking, made new covers for all the drawing room furniture. A considerable amount of furniture was also bought at Mount View and left in place. The dining room, too big for daily use by our more moderately sized twentieth-century family, was furnished with a very large table and immense Victorian sideboards. I have happy memories of amazing teas served there when we had tennis parties: always 'splits' (plain bread rolls), not scones in those days, with lots of Devonshire clotted cream and jam, as well as cake and perhaps chocolate biscuits. As teenagers not even this prevented us from returning enthusiastically to the tennis court for a further two or three sets. I choose to attribute to this conditioning my continuing ability, on my occasional visits to England, to indulge in more than one 'cream tea' without harmful consequences.

The tennis court was the fulfilment of another of my father's dreams. There was only one space in the garden level enough (apparently an old archery range) but I am sure he had taken note of the space before ever purchasing the house. As soon as he could, he employed an out-of-work cousin to lay a well-drained foundation and had an all-season hard court built.

Mount View did not disappoint us. During the short nine years granted us before war changed our lives we made great use of our dream house as a family, and each in his or her own way. Mount View's outstanding characteristic was not luxury but liveability, and the capacity to provide occupation for each of us that seemed meaningful and was certainly enjoyable. Of course, family problems did not vanish overnight. I could paint a whole picture of the tensions and struggles that arose in our family, as in every family. But here I will focus on the blessings of those years.

Although the new house was scarcely 15 minutes' drive from the hospital, perhaps 20 minutes from his consulting rooms, some of Harold's colleagues assured him that moving to the edge of town would be the kiss of death to his practice, that separating his consulting rooms from his residence was extremely unwise, that he would be seen as inaccessible – indeed, all round, that he would come to regret this big step.

Harold had more good sense than to listen to them. Ever since his student days, he had pined for the country, for outdoors, for regular exercise. Now he could come home at night, change into old clothes and saw logs for the fireplace, mend something, or find time and an opponent for a game of tennis. A great delight for me was to hold the other end of the cross-cut saw. We did not talk much but I felt deeply peaceful companionship.

I do not know how Harold felt about not sharing his wife's bedroom (they had long had separate beds). There was a dark side here; he had never shaken off his puritanical parents' belief in sex as only a means to procreation (they had procreated a dozen). On her part, Jo never gave any indication (that I saw) of finding or expecting enjoyment from sex. In later life Harold sometimes bemoaned his sinfulness. I am convinced that what he referred to was his carnal desires, not any extra-marital – or even marital? – fulfilment of them. Luxury my mother enjoyed and her room was more than comfortable. At his wish, my father's, for the rest of his life, was simple and starkly furnished, almost as bare as a monastic cell. What he needed was there, nothing more. The dressing gown that had been given him on his marriage hung on his bedroom door, so threadbare you could almost see through it, until his death in the 1960s.

What Jo needed more than anything was a purpose and an occupation. Mount View gave her both. Undoubtedly, it also fed a quite snobbish streak in her, but this was less important. When she had finished overseeing the redecorating to her satisfaction, she set to work on the garden. All along the side of the new tennis court she created a broad 'herbaceous border', very much in vogue at the time. All that the term meant was 'a garden of perennials' – lupins, delphiniums, irises, hollyhocks, gladioli, many others whose names I never knew bloomed in glory, were admired by the tennis players, were traded or propagated by cuttings or spare bulbs, occasionally created bad feelings (this garden enthusiast was jealous, that one was selfish) but more often created joy to be shared. Old Miss Marian's one ageing gardener, whose unfortunate name was Frost, was provided with assistance until he retired and was replaced.

Another of my mother's garden projects was the creation of a separate small area of crazy paving, also near the tennis court – and also in style at the time. She had a load of special colourful flat pieces of rock delivered, and she did much of the work of setting them in place herself – with more than a little help from Nannie. This was not the kind of cemented-in-place crazy paving more common now, but consisted of stones with sufficient earthy space between for carefully chosen tiny plants to grow. I loved it.

The Mount View garden abounded in flowers that came up untended. Although some rare plants had succumbed to overcrowding and the inadequate resources of the old gardener, many had survived. The southwestern corner of the UK enjoys a near Mediterranean climate, warm and damp, and our garden was full of magnolias, camellias, multi-coloured primula, rambling roses and daffodils that just came up or flowered anew in abundance every year. My mother 'did the flowers' almost daily. Although I felt she despised any feeble efforts I made (I never remember any praise from her), I certainly inherited her love for home-grown cut flowers and whenever I have been settled enough to have as much as a tiny balcony, I have rejoiced in planting and harvesting annuals – pansies, nasturtiums, cosmos, petunias, marigolds, whatever is available. Even then, at the age of ten, flowers seemed to me a wonderful enhancement of anyone's life. When some tea-time visitor of my mother's was leaving, I would ask them if they would like to take some daffodils home, and would rush off to cut from our abundance. A great joy, in the spring that came so early to the southwest, was to pick several small bunches of flowers – violets, primroses, grape hyacinths, others whose names I scarcely knew – and, with Nannie's help, pack them in moist moss and mail them off to my mother's eldest sister, beloved Aunt Lizzie, as a harbinger of the spring that would not reach her Scottish home for a full month yet. It is hard to believe now in the speed and efficiency of the postal service that enabled this. Technology advances, but you cannot email spring flowers.

My parents had always done a certain amount of entertaining, of having guests to dinner. Mount View enabled more of this, in addition to the more relaxed tennis parties. One year, while I was away at school, the British Medical Association held its annual conference in Plymouth, and my parents hosted a garden party.

The older of my brothers, Douglas, benefited less than the rest of us from Mount View because he was already in his late teens and less often at home. But he enjoyed the tennis court, enjoyed bringing his friends from medical school to Mount View. I have warm memories of one of these young men, who took time out to help me with my current major project – I was building myself a rustic little house deep in the wooded part of the garden, and Douglas's friend spent the better part of a day finding long logs for the framework and setting them in place. I planned to make the walls of interwoven bamboo. Although my little house was never finished, it was a special place to me. Much as it owed to Douglas's friend, it owed more to my father's lack of sexism and his more than willingness to let his 10 to 12 year old daughter use a sharp knife and a sharp small axe, and to trust her to chop away at the bamboo plantation with reasonable judgement and no supervision. He knew that safety lay in practising the proper use of tools, not in staying away from them. Climbing trees was also positively encouraged – and there were plenty of tall, inviting ones.

I think Douglas may have felt some envy of George and me, who had more of a stake in the place. But, although we had lived in town in his (Douglas's) childhood, our father had even then ensured as much country time as possible for all of us. Douglas was the only one of us to own a horse – first, a tubby Dartmoor pony called Bay Sahib (Britain was highly imperial in those days) and later the hunter Watchful, each in turn boarded at country stables. George and I learned to ride, but never well enough to avoid Douglas's disparagement.

George, too, was at boarding school long before we went to Mount View, and moved on from his preparatory school to equally or even more unpleasant experiences at his public school at about the same time as the move took place. I remember sensing a real unseen gap between us when he first returned from public school; and at the time he did not tell me anything much about what it was like. But he was soon the same old close playmate.

I am not sure whether the extent to which George and I were dependent on each other's company – and enjoyed it – was unusual in those days. I don't think it ever struck our father as out of the ordinary. In his childhood, families had been large – he was one of 12 – and all the children largely relied on the siblings closest in age for company, with occasional extended visits to or from members of some other vast family of cousins. As long as we were outdoors, well exercised and not quarrelsome, he was happy with our condition. Together we climbed trees, played clock golf, tennis and bicycle polo, and in really bad weather, we played table tennis or, occasionally, billiards.

We were not evenly matched. George, two and a half years older, was much better at almost everything. We fell into a system, devised perhaps by ourselves, perhaps initially by a wise adult, by which George just automatically imposed a handicap on himself. If I began a game of ping-pong with a 5-point advantage, we would often be even at 20-20 and – the handicap forgotten – would enjoy fierce competition for the final victory. I have thought of this often, when I have heard all competition condemned, or when I have found it over-praised. Of course, we sometimes quarrelled. I remember one particular fight, over a clock golf score. Ironically, the competition was in self-righteousness (were we rather priggish?). George maintained that I was leading, I that he was. I became so angry that I could easily have done him serious injury; and I was utterly humiliated when I looked up to see one of Douglas's girlfriends, a young woman on whom I had quite a crush, watching from the window. I have been angry many times since, often with more cause, but I do not remember many times when I have been, for a few minutes, so completely out of control.

Most of our time was spent in imaginative games, in which George was – as I remember it – always the leader. Our games used to take off and last a whole season, often more. George built me a little box car to drive around the paths which ran through our garden. It began as a four-wheeler, a board and two axles, but he built on to it a little car, painted blue, with a seat, a hand brake and perhaps a steering wheel. However, it did not last long in this elegant incarnation and was soon again stripped down to the four-wheels-and-a-board design, steered by the feet. It was

George, Tony and yet another vehicle

quickly joined by a second similar vehicle. We now had the materials for a game that lasted through the holidays of at least a couple of years. Almost the whole garden was on a slope, some paths were steep and winding, one led down precipitously to the bottom of the old landscaped quarry (euphemistically called the Dell) from which the stone for the house must have come. We named them all, rated them according to the hazard they presented, and devised challenging tests, races and competitions. We had at the time the use of a decrepit old typewriter on which we typed up tests and certificates to be awarded when the tests were passed, ranging from Learners to Racing Drivers. We also had the loan of a proper stop watch. A young man who visited and was rash enough to take part, asked us whether there had perhaps been any more siblings, who had not survived. Well, he had landed on a silver cigarette case in his back pocket when he fell off, leaving both it and himself rather the worse for wear. We did try to warn visitors – but it was fun when they participated. I could never measure up to George in daring and skill in this game (I do not think I ever mustered the courage for the breakneck descent into the Dell), but George never put me down. When we reminisced together in our eighties, I was startled to find myself glowing when he spoke of having been proud of my courage.

There was a small cottage on the property, intended for occupation by the gardener. But when we had a gardener with a family, my father preferred to pay him a bit more and let the cottage stand vacant. The front door opened directly on to the road, and although it was a private road serving only the school and half a dozen houses, he was not prepared to take the risk of having a small child run out the door into the

I was very much at home in George's outgrown shorts

path of a delivery van. So one year George and I had the use of the cottage as a play house. I remember the games that year less well and with less unalloyed pleasure. We were into early adolescence by then, but not ready to put aside our childish games, George's hormones inclined him to more macho imaginings. We played out James Bond kind of adventure stories, brandishing toy guns and climbing in and out of windows (safer than that hazardous front door, perhaps). But I was sometimes conflicted, grateful that I was usually cast as one of the cops or one of the robbers; I would have been insulted to be expected to play a shrinking maiden. But at the same time I wanted to make the cottage cosy and homelike, even if only for the benefit of the imaginary heroes we impersonated. Even at his most macho, George was a gentle soul. How lucky I was to have his companionship. School holidays, when he came home, were lit up by the good times we had together. No one in our family had more ownership in the delights of Mount View, or benefited more from the move than I.

A new friend had come into my life just before the move to Mount View. Wise friends of my parents – a doctor and his wife, with whom we visited quite often, and who, I think, also felt themselves in debt to my father for the removal of an appendix or some such – talked my parents into allowing them to give me a small dog. Tony, a Sealyham, was about 6 months old when he arrived, a most loving puppy, with great personality and a palpable sense of humour. We adored each other. The loneliness that occasionally affected me when George was at school was partially mitigated by Tony, who was with me all day, every day, enjoyed the garden as much as I did, and was there, warm and amenable to being cuddled whenever I needed him. The English are noted for being sentimental about their dogs. Looking back, it strikes me that the cuddleability of Tony may have filled a desperate need in me, growing up in a culture (and a family) in which humans displayed very little physical affection towards one another.

Periodically, Nannie bathed Tony, a process he hated, in the second bathroom. Normally, he never went off into the garden without me, although the front door usually stood open in fine weather. But if Nannie began to run the big bath in the second bathroom at an unusual time of day, Tony would get up quietly and slip away downstairs and out the door, to pay an unexpected visit to the gardener. On one rare occasion, when Douglas rode Watchful to the edge of town and turned up at the front door of Mount View on horseback, Tony was consumed by jealousy of the attention paid to the horse, and snuck around to nip his heel – he was lucky not to be sent flying over the rockery.

Tony loved to go in the car, no matter where, but especially to picnics or on country drives. The word 'car' would excite him. Understandably, he hated it when any of us went back to school. When one of the big school trunks was brought down from the attic, he went on high alert. During loading, if the car door was left open for even a few minutes (more common in those days, when the car was not programmed to beep or scream at you on every excuse), he would slip quietly out of the house and try to conceal his little body somewhere in the vehicle. If one of us had to go, why could he not go too?

Mary Daukes and Nannie after tennis

Tony felt taller and closer to his humans when sitting up

We moved to Mount View in the summer; the egregious Miss Straw was dismissed and departed, unmourned by me. In the fall, I started to attend a private day school called Moorfield, about a 20-minute walk away. Nannie usually took me there and back on foot. After a while I walked alone. In very bad weather my father's driver or my mother would fetch me by car.

Education is still heavily class-bound in Britain. Before the reforms that followed the Second World War, it was much more so. More than fear of having children make socially undesirable friends or acquire the 'wrong' accent kept professionals from sending their children to public elementary schools. Free education virtually dead-ended at age 15. The only route from state-sponsored elementary schools to secondary education was through a hard-won scholarship place. Plenty of room existed for good, bad and indifferent private schools to accommodate the children of all aspiring parents who could afford the fees.

It is probably ridiculous for me to presume to pass judgement on Moorfield (where I attended for a scant two years almost eighty years ago), but memoirs are licenced to make such presumptions, and I comfortably grade it as slightly on the better end of 'indifferent'. There were good teachers and not-so-good teachers; sensible and unnecessary rules; a rather feeble attempt at school spirit; many attempts to motivate by competition; and a somewhat lukewarm ethics, designed more to make sure parents remained satisfied than to foster any real understanding of co-operation and justice.

I remember one incident. I was standing around in the playground one day, chatting with a girl called Angela, one of only a few boarders at the school, when with – as I recall – little or no provocation, she suddenly bit me on the arm, quite hard. Hard enough that when I took my dress off that evening, Nannie noticed the distinct mark left by Angela's sharp little teeth, and told my mother. She bundled me (dressed again) into the car and took me down to see the head mistress (Miss

Bailey), who sent for a scared-looking Angela who duly apologised. As far as I know – and as I very much hope – no very dire consequences for her followed. Why was I uneasy about this incident? I am still not sure. Was it because, inadvertently, I had broken the code against telling tales? Or was it because no one seemed remotely interested in what had pushed Angela into such atrocious behaviour – we were 10 years old, not infants, and we had not even been arguing, much less fighting? Or was it because – and I do remember being aware of this – there was such imbalance in the system. There I was with the support of the big people, my parents and Miss Bailey. There on the other side was one small Angela, whose parents were probably, like those of many of the boarders, on the other side of the world, serving in the military or colonial service, with their daughter seeing them only a few months every two or three years and, in between, waiting for their occasional letter. I had not in fact borne false witness against Angela, but if I had, it would still have been I who was believed. My parents' reaction was moderate and reasonable; but Angela had no advocate.

On the whole, I enjoyed being at school. Miss Straw had prepared me well. I was more than up to my age level academically. I remember the teacher asking how far each of us new students had gone in arithmetic. When I responded by naming things like 'Practice & Proportion', she did a double take and told me that yes, I was ahead of the class, but that all my terminology was out of date – 'we don't call it that now'.

Some subjects were new. I loved hearing the stories of Norse and Greek mythology and writing had long come quite easily. I don't think we did much art or handwork. My father's main interest in my schooling at this point was to make sure I wasn't worked too hard. I think he reluctantly accepted that I might do thirty minutes of homework before getting outdoors, certainly not more.

Carrying his belief to the extreme, in our first spring at Mount View, my father gave me an incalculable gift by taking me out of school for the whole term. My little dog and I explored Eden that spring. The reputation of old Miss Rooker had ensured that the whole grounds had seen virtually no human presence for years except that of old Mr. Frost, and had turned into a nature preserve, or at least a bird sanctuary (curiously, there were no animals, not even rabbits or the dreaded moles). I watched that spring leaf by leaf, green shoot by green shoot, bud by bud, nest by nest, bird's egg by bird's egg. At one point, I thought I would become knowledgeable by learning the names of the plants, taking as my source the enduring little metal plaques attached to the rarer shrubs by those gardeners from Kew many years previously. Unfortunately, these gave only obscure botanical names, and in Latin yet. I would recognise to this day a *symphoricarpos mollis* if I saw one, but nothing else, and it would have made much more sense to have known it by its common name of snowberry. I am happy to say that I soon gave up this pursuit and simply enjoyed each new revelation, calling everything by its simplest name, taught largely by Nannie. Alone in the garden, I crept under bushes, climbed trees, and disappeared inside a large round golden yew, where I shared the quiet, leafless centre with a hedge sparrow couple, raising their family from five tiny bright blue eggs. Overwhelmed by beauty, I learnt what worship felt like.

Customarily, we took a family holiday every summer. Early in my childhood, these had always taken us to the Cornish seaside, to bathe in the sea and build sandcastles, and to live in lodgings not yet dignified by the name of 'bed and breakfast'. Later, we made trips to the coast of France, more interesting for my mother, and still satisfactorily provided with sand for us, and sometimes even with pony rides.

After the move to Mount View, my parents experimented with staying at home to enjoy our new home, but inevitably my father's vacation would be interrupted by the illness of a close friend who could not contemplate surgery done by anyone else. Even when we resumed holidaying at a distance, my father felt the need to protect himself from the freeloaders who, as soon as they learnt that he was a doctor, would describe their symptoms to him at great length. His secretary forwarded letters in batches in big brown envelopes, with no identifying designations (such as his accustomed 'FRCS'). On one holiday, when we were staying on the Island of Mull, I remember my father practically hissing at the hotel concierge who addressed him as 'Doctor'. Ironically, his cover was truly blown on that holiday because Nannie developed an abscess under a fingernail, and my father had to lance it, with the aid of the local doctor, to the great excitement and admiration of the small hotel community.

Fishing for trout, Mull

68

George and I remembered, throughout all our long lives, that holiday on Mull as the best of all times. Tobermory lies on the shore of a small bay, protected from the open sea by an island across its mouth. My mother, taking Nannie with her, spent most of her days fishing for trout on a nearby loch, under the guidance of a Scottish ghillie. George and I were allowed to rent a rowboat and go wherever we wanted around the bay, exploring the coastline, landing here and there. Sometimes my father came with us, more often he went with my mother, or just enjoyed his leisure on his own. One day, when there was a brisk breeze, after I had rowed out to the middle of the bay, George held up his raincoat and we came partway home under wind power. At lunch time we dug into Nannie's possessions and extracted an old sheet she used for ironing (all holidays were in part working holidays for her, I fear) and set up a sail, bearing a splendid emblem in the shape of a scorch mark shaped like a flatiron.

Sometimes George and I caught mackerel in the bay, but, while the hotel would cook respectable trout for its guests for next morning's breakfast, mackerel were not deemed worthy. My parents became good friends with the manager, a somewhat ill-fitting transplant from a big town. It was the custom to display any sizeable trout before dinner. On one occasion my mother removed the exhibit labelled 'The Manager's catch' and replaced it with a sardine lifted from that evening's hors d'oeuvres.

Iona Abbey, with live deerhound

Another highlight in that holiday was a day-long family trip to the far end of Mull and across the water by small motorboat to Iona Island – no ferry then. I think restoration of the mediaeval Abbey had barely begun, and tourists were few. The Abbey fulfilled all and more of its promise, not

69

Iona Abbey painted by the author 80 years later

only as a romantic ancient site, but much more authentically as a place of quiet faith and beauty. I have never forgotten the warm colourful rock of which it was built. George helped me take a photograph of the simple interior on black and white film on my elementary Ensign box camera, whose one fancy trick was that it was possible to hold the shutter open for the few seconds needed to take an interior image. There were no coloured glass windows at that time, and of course, no colour film to snap them in, but the scene was dramatically enhanced by a live deerhound, lying as if carved from stone at the foot of one of the pillars. I recently made a much larger watercolour image from this small picture. The peace and the ambience of Iona have stayed with me, something mystical perhaps, not so much brought there so long ago by the monks as found there by them, and still there for the finding.

That summer, I had also fitted in a two-week trip to the Lake District, to work in a very small YWCA camp I had heard about from someone at school. The girls there were drawn from the poorest areas of those Cumberland industrial towns hardest hit by the Depression. A dozen or so girls slept in the small church in the Newlands Valley or in a tent outside. The younger girls in particular had a hard

Iona Cathedral postcard

70

YWCA Girls' Camp, Newlands Church, Cumberland 1937

time overcoming simple fear of being out in the unfamiliar countryside. I was encouraged by the leaders to get to know the older girls, who were close to me in age, but oh, so different from me in experience. We walked and talked together, often climbing quite a long way on the steep hillsides. Poorly shod, unhealthy, and unaccustomed to the countryside, the few I got to know toiled up hills uncomplaining, and told me something of their lives. None were still in school. Those who were fortunate enough to have a job worked at food shops or restaurants, and, as I recall, were often employed to take meals to businessmen at their desks – and to dodge their sexual attentions. I am not sure that I had ever heard of such hazards before. In the evenings, the two leaders and I sat together to chat, and I think they, rightly, saw it as their job to educate me with some picture of the seamier side of life. I was, and am, grateful for the widening of my vision.

Many years later, the Newlands Valley came to be familiar to me in a completely different context, when I became involved in studying the life of Catherine Marshall, the leading suffragist and peace activist whose home was at Hawse End, a big house a short distance from the Newlands Church. I often wonder whether the camp could have been an initiative of hers – it would have appealed to her – and I can even fantasise that she came by one day to see how we were doing. But this is not supported

71

A picnic was always better with a river

by any clear memory, let alone evidence.

Next year we went to Ulster, staying in a hotel near the sea, at the foot of the Mountains of Mourne. To our disappointment, no local entrepreneur rented out rowing boats. The holiday took a very different turn. George was seventeen, an approach to adulthood that manifested in his having just got his driving licence, and in his falling in love with Wendy, a fifteen-year old who was staying in the same hotel, with her brother and her mother, the latter attended by a faithful male escort. We were quite often blessed with use of the car, and became familiar with the roller-coaster roads of Northern Ireland. Wendy's brother Bill and I were not attracted to each other, but George dearly and innocently loved Wendy, a passion that would last long. She had a hard life; her mother cared little for her, somewhat more for her brother, and a great deal for herself.

It would be absurd to pretend that all the good things of my childhood were unalloyed. In fact, for many years, the dark side was more present with me. In particular, I remember feeling quite unhappy much of the time before the move to Mount View, perhaps mainly because I found it so hard to please my mother. Even at Mount View there were, of course, bad times, times when I sensed tension between my parents, times when I was lonely, and a good many times when I was a thoroughly grumpy teenager. My mother was not skilled at dealing with an adolescent daughter, and I am sure I was difficult. A tomboy, careless of my appearance, often ungracious with strangers, I was so far from being the daughter she wanted. She still lost her temper at times and not only would we shout at one another but she would try to spank me, an absurd but humiliating encounter which would leave me sobbing and defeated. One such contretemps was witnessed by a friend visiting from boarding school.

After that episode I vowed to myself that I would always hate my

mother. Now I wish I had not kept
this vow as long and as bitterly as
I did. In my contented old age I
prefer to recall the good times,
and they were many. More and
more, too, I have come to
empathise with my mother's
difficulties and especially to wish
that we had been better able to
understand each other. Looking
back, I see a lot that I like about
her. At her best, she was witty,
mischievous, adventurous and
generally supportive of any out-of-
the ordinary things I wanted to
do. She was one of the best
boarding-school mothers, sitting
down with absolute regularity
once a week to write a newsy

*George with Wendy Fletcher and a lamb,
Dartmoor*

letter to each of her children. Although in general I longed for more
tenderness from her, if ever I was ill she reverted to being a nurse, a
caring as well as an efficient nurse. During a measles epidemic in which
the demand for nurses at boarding schools outran the supply, she
horrified me by volunteering at my school, but proved in the event to be
well-liked as well as efficient.

I think my parents were good employers. Most of their staff stayed
long, Nannie of course longest of all. My father's secretary was a trained
nurse. She regularly took lunch with us while we lived at Lockyer Street
but we saw less of her after the move to Mount View. There were a cook
and two maids before the move; only a cook and so-called parlour-maid
after it. They did come and go from time to time, but not frequently. I
have no recollection of whoever looked after the cars when we lived
downtown, although I am sure my father had at least a part-time
mechanic who also served as an occasional driver. After the move a
young man called Northcote was employed full-time, helping out in the
garden on a regular basis, as well as looking after the cars. He was
officially designated as chauffeur-mechanic, but the chauffeur part –
when he donned a cap and minimal uniform – was probably the least of
his work. Harold liked to drive himself – fast – and would never be
driven to a case, though occasionally, if he was very tired, he was glad to

take Northcote along to drive him home. None of the family expected or wanted to be driven around, although, rarely, I might be fetched from school.

We had a full-time gardener, also assisted by a part-time man, ex-navy, called Martin (Pincher Martin, of course, in accordance with navy custom). The garden included a very large kitchen patch, so they all worked hard, and they had some fun, too. They held my father in great respect, some of the neighbours less so, one in particular who was regarded as putting on airs. Mr. Randall clearly liked to see himself as a country squire – though neither the size nor location of any of the properties down our road warranted this – and he told my father that he would never demean himself by manual labour. I felt too that he considered women, his own and others, as lesser beings. Mr. Randall owned a red setter, a beautiful dog that had been rendered timid and ineffectual by brutal training, and he owned a gun. With dog and gun, he liked to parade his status. He was, I suppose, a good shot. One morning he shot two pigeons. Inevitably, they flew across the road from his small garden and fell to the ground among our trees. He sent his dog in to retrieve them, but the men – who always knew the letter of the law when they could score by it – set my small Tony (who needed little encouragement) after the big red setter, which turned tail and fled. The men picked up the pigeons and very correctly offered them to my mother, who declined them. All were agreed that a nice pigeon pie would make a treat for Martin's tea, so at the end of the day they were tied on to his bicycle handle bars. To make sure that poor Mr. Randall got the full benefit of their triumph, they called out loudly as Martin was passing his house 'Hey, Pincher, you got them pigeons?'

If I wanted to express my memories of Mount View during the seven years we had before the war in terms of colours and abstract shapes, the colours would be bright green, yellow, a warm orange – and a peaceful blue; the shapes would be curved, triangular, flowing yet substantial, solid, secure. Once war arrived, at first imposed on these patterns and ultimately displacing them, I see jagged, angular black and red, flashes of glowing white, jerky movement, and at the core, a closeness and warmth that yet lacks security.

CHAPTER 6

Boarding School

In prewar Britain education was a prime keeper of the class system. To describe someone as 'educated' was similar to declaring them to be 'gentry', another term now going out of use – perhaps as too blatantly classist. A man described as educated was assumed to be the product of a public school, that is, of an emphatically private school, unless of course he was of the aristocracy when he just might have been educated by tutors at home. Much the same categorisation applied to women, though the range of private institutions was more varied.

A handful of the best-known girls' schools liked to be known also as 'Public Schools', and modelled themselves on their male counterparts, with – of course – the increased restrictions which were expected in the care of girls. Overall, as I see it, the saddest mistake in private girls' education was this tendency to emulate the male tradition, instead of taking advantage of the comparative freedom to change and improve. Books could be written on this, but not by me. Downe House, to which I had the great good fortune to be sent, was the creation of one woman and at that time still her property. Olive Willis did not share the fear of innovation, but struck a fine balance between tradition and thought-out difference. Nor was she over-protective. Rules were few and aimed at maintaining comfortable living in community, good health, and serious attention to study. The focus was on education in a true sense, not on academic achievement only, not on sports only, not on arts and music

The dormitory buildings at Downe House

75

only, and certainly not primarily on training us to be good wives for the products of the boys' public schools. I have to admit that I now recognise Miss Willis was something of an elitist, truly thinking we were of finer stuff than the general population. But she made sure we had no excuse to think that that entitled us to anything but increased responsibility for making good use of our opportunities, to the benefit of others, not just of ourselves.

None of this philosophising, of course, was part of the thinking of the twelve-year-old me when I first entered the school. But Miss Willis was much given to telling stories and giving what could have been called little homilies, had they not been so free of pretension. She never encouraged us to think of ourselves as delicate. I remember how delighted she was to tell the tale of several recently graduated students who, finding themselves for some reason confronted with a whole massive catch of herring in danger of spoiling, had set to and gutted the lot.

Very shortly after I arrived at Downe, I heard Miss Willis weigh in against a slogan that I fancy had been initiated by Arthur Mee, editor of *The Children's Newspaper*, a slogan that had grown almost into a campaign, welcomed, and dinned approvingly into children by most adults, including some in my life. The phrase was 'SAFETY FIRST', and to hear my new headmistress state emphatically that this was not an attitude to live by was thought-provoking, a freeing experience. I learnt both that it might be proper to want to live adventurously, and that adults did not all share a common repressive philosophy.

My parents' choice of Downe House was a great gift to me. For a long time I thought that it came from good luck rather than good judgement, but now I think that may have been a characteristic teenage injustice. During their search for a school for me, they visited several well-known schools, and must, I think, have come to Downe on a sunny summer Sunday. My father surely loved the school's rural hilltop location; he was pleased to see girls sitting around outside in informal groups; he was delighted to learn that we had individual freedom to roam in a substantial acreage of woodland. He and my mother probably both liked the smaller bedrooms that took the place of the large cubicle-lined dormitories they saw in other schools. My mother will have appreciated the individual clothing worn out of school hours and the access to a variety of fine arts. All this, and a commitment to academic achievement leading to good public examination results and university entrance.

Both valued education highly. My mother had followed a career until late marriage. My father had already made the decision, rare at that time, that I would have the same opportunities as my brothers. Perhaps what I did not give my parents credit for was their acceptance of the risk of sending me to a school dedicated to encouraging us to think for ourselves, to become our own persons. I wish that we had talked more at home about ideas. I might have found I had more in common with my parents than I thought, and perhaps more acceptance of our differences than I ever dared look for.

But what the undersized twelve-year-old who was dropped off at the school halfway through the Lent term of 1935 was concerned with was the unfortunate circumstance of being the only 'new girl'. I arrived at half term because a few days before the term properly began, in January, I had fallen ill with a virulent flu and pneumonia. I remember the illness well; I was desperately sick. As a child of the medical community I was well looked after, at home, though there was little that could be done in those pre-antibiotic days. One of my clearest recollections was of looking up from my bed at a circle of my mother, my father, and another eminent doctor, conferring earnestly about what to do. A tiny fourth figure had joined the circle – my little dog, Tony, sitting upright on his rear end in the 'begging' position, looking anxiously from one face to another.

All that expertise, or knowledge or skill, or a good constitution, or Tony's faithful love had prevailed, but slowly. When the fever went down, I was surprised by the sight of my wasted legs, bony with a flap of flesh hanging where my firm calves had been. Recovery was slow and did not really begin until one teatime I was suddenly tempted by the four tiny marmite sandwiches offered to me. Perhaps this explains my lifetime devotion, inexplicable to many, to that strange salty brown spread.

My first half term was not easy. Miss Willis sometimes mixed up her endeavours to do the best for everyone. The school was slightly overcrowded. There was a woman who lived on the edge of the school's woodland who was in financial need: several of us, supposedly those who would benefit from extra care, were allocated to her as boarders. Looking back, I wonder if Mrs. F actually concealed the fact that her husband had active tuberculosis. I am sure my father never knew – nor, for that matter did I until much later, though I remember him as feverish and ill. But Mrs. F certainly presented a different picture of herself to Miss Willis than she showed to us. She was not the warm, caring person Miss Willis thought her. She was not definably cruel, just rather unkind, given for instance to making disparaging remarks about any of our parents who she felt had not contributed adequately to the supply of candy to be shared in the evenings. For me, the biggest difficulty, for which I can hardly blame her, was that we had to rush to her house after afternoon games, change into our after-school clothes, put our sports shoes back on and run through the woods so as to be back in time to change into house shoes for the evening homework period. Speed has never come easily to me, and I frequently earned a reprimand for my tardiness. Five years later, when I was a school senior, I and some others who had shared the experience spoke up when Miss Willis was consulting with us about room placement for the new students expected the following term. (And what other headmistress ever consulted students in such a way? and why had not previous seniors spoken of the problems we had found?) She quickly found another role for Mrs. F.

Despite such small setbacks, I enjoyed boarding school almost unreservedly, although in Canada it is almost an embarrassment to admit it. If I search my mind, I do recall a few bad patches when I couldn't make friends with my roommates, when I was confined to the sick bay for no good reason, when I disliked the gym instructor's methods, when one or other class seemed boring. But overall, my body was healthy, my mind was expanding, work was interesting and varied; I had friends and more freedom than I had at home.

My earlier childhood might have been designed to ensure that making friends was not easy for me, although this never occurred to my parents. In our walks on Plymouth Hoe we were not allowed to speak to strangers of any age. After we moved and I entered day school, I rarely brought a classmate home. I did have two or three quite good friends in Plymouth, found for me mostly by my parents, and able to be visited or to visit only by parental arrangement. As we moved into our teens, our acquaintance widened, but not a great deal.

My first close friend at Downe, whom I still recall with affection, left unexpectedly for health reasons. For a while I hung out with an unhappy youngster, one of the relatively few who never did settle down. She was, I think now, mentally disabled in some way, and later became an embarrassment to her very prominent family when she became involved in some criminal activity. Miss Willis's efforts to integrate her included the rare privilege of stabling her own horse a mile or two from the school, and my companionship enabled her to visit the animal occasionally. Not realising her limitations, I tried to teach her a secret code I had invented, but only caused her some distress. I think I was thought to be 'good for her'. The truth was that I sought her out because at that time I too was lonely, and she was as good for me as I for her. I rather attracted those who were having difficulties. Another short friendship was with a girl who poured into my almost believing ear her lurid fantasies of a sado-masochistic relationship with a teacher we both admired. What I learnt from her – slowly and painfully – was that you must sometimes have reservations about what you are told, even while recognising that the teller believes it to be the truth.

Gradually I came to fit in with my classmates. The school's policy was to mix us all up as much as possible, revising dormitory allocations every term, mealtime tables twice a term, and always with a range of age. We were discouraged from having 'crushes'. Most of us conformed willingly, electing to see it as one of the ways in which we were superior to other schools. For me, it worked and I found good friends as I went through the school. I was always willing to speak up in class, and I may have taken part in unkind treatment of one or two less confident teachers. I remember one harmless prank I carried off for several weeks, conspiring with a friend or two to convince the visiting pottery teacher that I was twins, Jo and Jane, who inexplicably never both turned up to class at the same time. Our teacher was, I think, better at pottery than at reasoning.

One of the early joys of my first summer was that no one seemed to be trying to turn me into a lady. We, the younger ones, spent Saturday afternoons, unsupervised, climbing trees, sliding down the clay bank of a quarry or riding a Giant's Stride, a tall, sturdy pole with a number of cables attached to a rotating device on the top, sometimes called a Maypole Spinner. We hung on to the cable and wildly swung in circles around the pole. This device had been provided by Miss Willis when a local school complained that some Downe students were making too much use of theirs.

Later talking, talking became a prime pleasure, often facilitated by walking, walking. Other schools walked two by two, in 'crocodiles', under supervision. Whenever rain made our daily sports impossible, we had to put on our raincoats and go for a walk, in groups of three or more, chosen by ourselves. Miss Willis held that as long as there were three of us, we should be able to manage: 'One', she said, 'to have the accident, one to go for help, and one to stay with the body'. (My walks with my horse-owning friend had been permitted by a special dispensation from this rule.) Although I have to confess that my attention was more often focused on my companions rather than the scenery, I learnt to appreciate a landscape completely different from the open moorland and small hedged fields that had so long been my kind of countryside. Here we walked mostly in deep woodland, tall, ancient trees above, wet leaves underfoot.

Friendships were flexible at times; a spell in the sanatorium with measles, a fortuitous assignment of roommates, painting together in the Sketching Club, or acting in a school play, any of these things might open the way to a new friendship, not necessarily within the narrow ranks of one's own classmates. Some of these friendships endured long.

The time set aside daily for 'games' or for walking in the rain was at least two hours. In addition, almost every day's timetable included a forty-minute lesson period of gym or modern dance. There were a few complainers at all this obligatory exercise, but I loved it and thrived. I didn't shine, except for a brief period as a lacrosse goalie, helping the junior team to victory in Saturday afternoon matches against other schools, and thrilled to be several times among those read out for 'special mention', at Saturday supper time. But for some reason, puberty deprived me of the willingness to get in the way of hard rubber balls hurled at me – I started to dodge them, however much I tried not to. Instead of becoming a first team goalkeeper when I grew too old for the juniors, I barely hung on to a position in the third team, where I performed adequately, but no more. But I enjoyed daily practice games, especially as only one half of the time was spent in goal, to ensure that the goalies had exercise and did not freeze. Other games we played were netball, rounders, cricket and tennis. All this healthy activity, good food and lots of sleep doubtless contributed to the remarkable health I am blessed with in old age.

I have two regrets. Downe had a remarkable music programme, including optional tuition in many instruments, two orchestras, concert performances by distinguished musicians, and plenty of choral opportunities. I took very little advantage of any of this. I remember an audition, held by some of the senior singers, for permission to cut chapel choir practice. I never told anyone that I went to the audition hoping in my heart that I would fail, that I would be told that I really had a fine voice worth cultivating. Instead I was of course officially recognised as a 'growler' and excused from attendance. I am sure the assessment was merited, but the school was something of a music snob. If you arrived with no background, no effort was made to bring you up to speed. The egregious Miss Straw, claiming skill she did not have, had inculcated in me nothing but confusion and a dislike for piano lessons. In my last year at school, I begged my father for piano lessons, and received what proved to be quite a useful training in music appreciation, but little instruction in performance. My father, bless him, bought me a piano

which many years later made its way to South Africa to join me, and
suffered the surely unusual (and ultimately terminal) fate of being
dropped, not once, but twice, first on to the dock by those unloading it
from the ship, and secondly, by my husband and his friend, from a half-
ton truck. I minded more than I ever admitted.

My second regret is about tennis, or, to be more honest, about my lack
of moral courage. My father had laid down an all-weather hard court at
Mount View, and we all played tennis there and elsewhere, as a family,
at teenaged tennis parties, at adult tennis parties, and from time to time
in tournaments, where George and I were amicable partners. I loved it,
and became a strong player. Friends from other boarding schools would
say, 'you must be on your first team, surely'. But at school, I came to
recognise that the physical education teacher saw me as a game little
person completely lacking in athletic ability. My short success as a
lacrosse goalie understandably did nothing to change that, and that
opportunity had been mine only because the timing of my birthday
meant that I had one winter season as a junior. For tennis, my spring
birthday served me ill as I passed my thirteenth birthday before my first
summer term. Games lists were made out daily. We found our names
assigned to this or that tennis court, or a game of rounders or cricket. Day
after day, week after week, all summer term long, I was placed
somewhere on the distant field at cricket, or on the worst of the rabbit-
holed grass tennis courts, in the company of three (or worse still, only
two) of those who hated all games in general and tennis in particular.
These less-than-perfect courts, hidden in the woods, were seldom visited
by supervising staff, so even our lack-lustre and sometimes bad-tempered
games remained hidden, while the games teacher watched and coached
the promising players on the well-kept hard courts. Tennis coaching was
an extra, and although I enjoyed it and did well at it, the visiting coach
was not apparently consulted by the regular staff, or her advice was not
taken.

When there were inter-school matches, I volunteered as a ball girl, and
later as an umpire. This earned me yet more brownie points with the
phys. ed. teacher, but never suggested to her that perhaps I had a real
interest in the game – as a player. I watched the teams play, admired
their skill, and knew that I could have held my own with them. I could
only think of one, quite simple, solution: I must ask the teacher to give
me a chance to show what I could do. The staff room was a large, long
room, with an open passageway along one side. The form for speaking
to a staff member was to lie in wait in this passageway until you were

noticed and the attention of the teacher you wanted was drawn to you (a horrible arrangement for the staff, but they got quite good at not seeing the more tedious students). I went there, more than once, intending to speak to Miss Smith, formulating my pitch in my mind. But every time I backed off. What I was combating, and it seems ridiculous now, was the absolute bar we grew up with against the slightest self-praise. I simply could not find a way to say that I was quite a good tennis player without saying that I was quite a good tennis player, and I could not force those words out. Fear of rejection may have played a part, too. So I endured the painful, boring non-games to the end of my school days. For all that the school did for my self-confidence, I still had some serious problems.

As is proper and right, few of the shining memories of my first three years at school relate to classroom time, with the odd exception of finding – after a change of teachers – that math was comprehensible and enjoyable. Wonderful quirky moments stand out. High on my list is Miss Willis's practice, unexpected every year, of coming into the dining room at lunch time on that special day, usually some time in April, when spring suddenly arrives, and declaring that the rest of the day will be a holiday, and we are all to get outdoors and enjoy it in whatever way we choose. This disregard for their carefully prepared classes infuriated some of the teachers. But to this day that special spring day never passes without my memory glowing. What would I recall of anything I might have learned in class on those days?

Unlike other schools, we had an occasional whole day holiday at school, not for visits from or to parents. Miss Willis's birthday was one, and I rather think another, oddly, was Ascension Day (always a Thursday in spring). On these days we lined up after breakfast and were given a bag lunch – a sandwich, a hardboiled egg, an apple, perhaps a cookie, and presumably something to drink. Rain or shine, we then disappeared, in our threes and fours, not to be seen again until supper time.

One of the things my friends and I liked to do was walk to an old shed isolated in the middle of Bucklebury Common and seek out the man who made wooden bowls there. George Lailey had practised his craft all his life, as had his father and his father's father, and so on as far back as any could remember. He was the last of the Bucklebury bowlmakers, and is commemorated in H.V. Morton's *In Search of England*. Using a sapling for turning motion, and crude chisels made and sharpened by himself, Lailey turned bowls out, one from inside another, starting with a solid section of elm trunk. Always he told us he was working on a big order and was too busy to do any extras, always he yielded, and made one or two for us, finishing each by running a pencil around for decoration, and beeswax for protection of the edge, and finally putting his laboured signature in pencil on the base. He charged strictly by size, so the little ones we loved, that were probably most trouble to do, cost us about sixpence each, though we would also coax him to do a two-shilling salad bowl for some approaching maternal birthday. Mr. Lailey took pride in there being no waste from his production: the little knobs left from inside our small bowls went to support hats in milliners' shops, the shavings went for packing china. The bowls, he boasted, went by order all over the world. They were distinctive; sixty years later, coming on several in a National Trust house, I did not have to turn them over to know whose work they were.

Despite our unusual freedoms, much of our life was, appropriately, not open to choice. Attendance at class was obligatory, and so was going to chapel. The Anglicanism of the school was definite, though overlaid by idiosyncrasies of Miss Willis's own. Years later, I came to realise that we had a feminist example in the way our principal herself conducted our twice-daily church services, without benefit of ordination or the assistance of any male representative, with the one exception of holy communion, which was administered every few weeks early on a Sunday morning by an insignificant clergyman brought in – or should I say allowed in? – for the purpose (not that Miss Willis was anti-male; we had several men in part-time teaching positions, though this was rare in girls' schools). One or two other staff members occasionally conducted morning or evening chapel, and Sunday lessons, as prescribed in the Prayer Book, were read by students. Other than that all services were the provenance of Olive Willis, who preached, and led the service. Most of us were confirmed at about age fifteen, after instruction (again by Miss Willis), and of course a splendidly arrayed bishop had to be imported to conduct that service. When my cohort rose to the top of the school,

The Chapel

we once persuaded her to make Sunday evening chapel voluntary: she was devastated to find that more than half stayed away. What had she thought would happen? There was a gap in her broad vision in this area. I remember with embarrassment that she even put a lot of pressure (just short of compulsion, I am glad to say) on one Jewish refugee student to come to chapel. To her the opportunity was one of the greatest gifts she could give. She did not see how the young woman must see it as disloyal to her faith, the only thing of her own that she had been able to bring away from Nazi Germany with her.

For myself, chapel was in general no chore. I found it a peaceful time. I liked the music (despite my own inadequacy), and I often found Miss Willis interesting: and I suppose I wanted to be 'good'. Preparation for confirmation made me feel religious, and I liked to go alone to the chapel last thing at night to pray, though I was never quite sure what that meant.

The chapel: watercolour by my friend Ursula Pelly

I was glad that our services were free from frills – no incense, no candles – and I loved *Songs of Praise*, the up-to-date hymnbook from which we sang. I did not lack spiritual experience. As I have told, the garden at Mount View had brought me into touch with something beyond myself. I regret that I always felt under a compulsion to fit my deep sense of the

St Peter's, staff house, near to the school

mystical into the criteria of religion as taught. I had difficulty with the demand that I 'believe' a whole bunch of things of which I could have no knowledge. I experienced this mostly as a failure on my part. I did not have sufficient confidence in myself to realise that I did not have to accept the concept, so indeed I tried hard to feel a sense of belief.

One of the side benefits of being confirmed was that those who had taken this step were allowed to rise early on a Sunday morning and walk to whatever nearby village church we chose for communion, supplementing the meagre opportunities provided in the school chapel by the visiting clergyman. The three-at-a-time rule was even relaxed, so we could go with any one special friend. We understood that it was more holy to take communion fasting, but adolescent girls were somewhat prone to fainting, so cookies (a rare treat) were left out for us to pick up on our way out. In the cold wet winter months, I don't remember being driven forth by any enthusiasm for early morning communion, but I have radiant memories of walking to church in the summer, while the sun was still low and shadows were long, along the edges of fields where poppies and cornflowers mingled with the corn. I wonder if I ever reflected on the absurdity of going from this pure, exhilarating

Another view of St Peter's

experience into a small church and kneeling, prayer book open, to bewail my manifold sins and wickednesses.

Academically, I muddled happily along, in the higher section of each grade, passing in all but languages, but not ambitious. Teaching was more spotty in quality than it should have been. I finally came alive when our history class, preparing for the school certificate exams, was given over to the emergency care of Jean Rowntree, following the discovery that, by an administrative blunder, we had been studying the wrong syllabus. Jean normally only taught the post-certificate classes, the sixth form, but she brought her remarkable gifts to our aid. Rather than rushing through the syllabus in the too-short time left before the exam, she focused on the seventeenth century, and taught that in some depth. The decision to do it this way was based, I understand, not only on her own love of the seventeenth century, but on a careful analysis of the scope and arrangement of the expected exam papers, where the choice of questions was to be wide enough that we would be able to fulfil requirements within the more limited period we had been taught. It worked for us.

For the first time since Miss Straw, I began to think about how I wrote as well as just getting down on paper what the teacher was expecting. My very first short essay for Jean came back with about ten red marks indicating 'cliche'. Deeply shamed as I was, I was not the only offender, and we all benefited from the explanation and discussion that took place in class. Not incidentally, the text book used by our previous instructor had been full of expressions such as 'hardly was the ink dry on the treaty …' Now we were made more aware of style by being encouraged to look at the characteristics of seventeenth-century writing, or attempt an imitation of Samuel Pepys journal writing, or learn the use of the semi-colon. We received a boost, and considered it flattering, to find that Jean and her closest fellow teachers discussed our individual styles: one liked Ann's; one thought mine heavy, while Jean saw it as developing well.

Not only did Jean inspire interest and engagement, she was able at the same time to organise the material so that the notes we took were down-to-earth and provided a good outline for revision. Historical ideas, trends, personalities all became real to me for the first time, together with a minimal framework of dates and major events to fit them into, memorable for exam purposes, and a good model for future study. We came through the exam with satisfactory results. Oddly enough, in a general commentary provided to the school, the examiners did comment on the limited date range of our expertise, but they had, of course, to give

Ann Faber and Felicity Avern in The Shoemaker's Holiday

us credit, as the questions we chose to answer met all the printed requirements.

Although my results in the school certificate were inglorious, I had scraped together almost sufficient credits to qualify for university admission – that is, to obtain matriculation and to be allowed to sit the college entrance exams. All that was left was for me to raise my level a bit in languages, which could be done by repeating just these subjects. For some reason Miss Willis decided that it would be of more interest and value for me to sit the matriculation examination itself. Two others, Ann Faber and Virginia Dakin, were in the same boat, although I think their deficiencies were in different subject areas from mine. Looking back, I find it a strange decision; it imposed a new curriculum and a great deal of extra study on us, as we could not take just the subjects in which we needed to improve, but had to choose some new subjects as well to make up a complete package. So, starting from scratch, I studied the history of the Anglican Prayer Book, as well as redoing math – in which I had done quite well – and of course French and Latin

Meanwhile, most of the post-certificate class, of which we were a part, and which comprised some who were going on to university and some

'The Shoemaker's holiday' in the Greek outdoor theatre at Downe House. Jo (on the left) had the smallest part

who were not, was not studying any of the things we needed. Special tuition was set up for the Prayer Book course – which I came to find enjoyable. Ann, I think, had special tuition in math, and I must have had the same for Latin, which was no longer studied by the rest of the class.

How to get the help I needed in French, however, was a major problem. Customarily, after school certificate the class would embark on French literature, gladly leaving behind the basic grammar and syntax in which we needed coaching. Literature was taught by Mlle. Agobert, the most controversial teacher in the school, a fiery Parisian dreaded by all. Small and dark, she always wore black; indeed, we had it that she only owned two dresses, both black, wearing the one with a dark blue collar whenever she was in mourning, which was most of the time, and only graduating to the one with the tiny strip of white lace in the rare happy times when no one of her extended – and extensive – family had died for at least a year. She was thought to be a great teacher; why, I am not sure. She loved her subject and she had a dramatic flair, but this was less often employed on her subject matter than it was on enhancing her own reputation. We were all terrified of her. I had made up my mind that she would never make me cry – and she never did. But she was cruel and mean. For some reason, Ann Faber, not quite as skinny as the rest of us, and a little careless at times, was a chosen target. Mlle. Agobert always had our homework returned to us in the dining room at teatime. All homework was done in small exercise books, one for each subject, Agobert demanded perfection: no erasures, no torn out pages, no corrections – just writing it was stressful. Ann was subject to small accidents; in the next class Agobert would bang on her desk, throw the chalk at her and shout, 'Ann Faber, you 'ave jam on your book, you are fat and lazy, a pig' and go into a tirade that would last for minutes.

Despite these frequent episodes Ann was not the only victim – all the class was looking forward to studying French literature, and would be furious if Mlle. Agobert decided instead to teach what we needed for our matriculation preparation. I was between a rock and a hard place, but I found what I hoped was a working solution by going to one of the other French teachers and asking for private coaching. We conspired not to tell Mademoiselle. But of course she found out. I went innocently to the third class of the literature course. After ten minutes of reasonably peaceful study of Corneille, Mlle. Agobert picked up the lid of her desk and banged it down, causing the whole class to jump. She turned on me; 'Josephine Vellacott', she spat out, 'You 'ave deceived me!' This time the tirade lasted not five minutes but the entire period, and was repeated next time the class met. So my classmates lost their literature study anyway. At the end of this second onslaught, Agobert, declaring me unworthy even to open the door for her, flounced out, declaring she was going to Miss Willis to resign.

I made a strategic decision and rushed off to tell Miss Willis my side of the story before she got hers in. Miss Willis agreed that my attempt at secrecy had been unwise, but she was used to dealing with Mademoiselle's tantrums, and indeed, with her resignations. Whether it was on this occasion or some other issue a little later, Miss Willis decided she had had enough of the histrionics and startled Mademoiselle by accepting her resignation. So, as it happened, Mlle. Agobert was in Paris when it fell to Hitler, and I believe, turned her talents to making life hard for the occupying troops.

The last two years of school were the time when the deepest friendships were formed. My cohort included Ann Faber and Virginia Dakin, two who were studying alongside me for the Somerville College entrance exam. Virginia was the only child of a widowed mother whose home was South Africa. I think to this day that Virginia may have been the most able of us all, but she had no public face at all. She never spoke in class unless in response to a direct question, seldom smiled and was as near to invisible as she could be. Only very gradually, as we came to know each other in a small group, did she show herself as not only bright but witty. She also took excellent notes and wrote well. It is a mystery to me why the teachers did not draw her out more. She and I and Ann Faber formed a close bond, able to talk endlessly.

As a friend, Ann Faber widened my cultural horizon. That sounds pompous, but her background opened the door for me to a world far from the one I had grown up in. Ann's father, Geoffrey Faber, owned and ran Faber, the up-and-coming publisher of the thirties. In the sixth form, we were introduced to modern poetry by a new teacher, Nancy Medley, and behold, our textbook was *The Faber Book of Modern Verse.* Gerard Manley Hopkins spoke to me as none of the classic poets had. I still have my copy of the Faber book, rather the worse for wear, but hardbound and printed on high quality cream coloured paper. Name-dropping was not liked at Downe, and Ann said little in class about the literary figures that peopled her home world and family conversation, much as appendices and gallstones inhabited mine.

One summer Virginia and I together spent a couple of weeks with the Fabers at their holiday place. Ann's younger brothers, Dick and Tom, lent us their bicycles and we rode wildly up and down the steep hills of

Wales, nothing unfamiliar in that kind of activity. But in the evenings we all settled down in the living room to take turns in reading from Dickens, and one of the circle of readers was T.S. Eliot. He was then at the height of his fame, and quite dominant in that textbook of ours, but known to the Faber children as Old Possum, honorary Uncle Tom. Shortly afterwards (1939) Faber published Eliot's *Old Possum's Book of Practical Cats*, dedicated to the Faber children. He was, I think, deeply grateful for the privacy that such family times provided. I can't say that we came to know him well, but I have occasionally since told friends that my claim to fame rests on having gone shrimping with T.S. Eliot, which was also something we did.

The other things I remember about that holiday are the lateness of the servantless evening meal, washing up afterwards – and being bidden to use cold water for the glasses – and my own unsuccessful efforts to persuade Virginia to take part in the reading, which I knew she could do well. Ann's mother, Enid (nee Richards, and a Downe graduate) was also a new experience for me. Married at sixteen, she had been in her teens when Ann was born, so much younger than my mother. She was always good to me, and I came to love her. Although it was so much more modern a family than mine, women were in reality accorded less equality than my father strove to make part of our household. Preparation of the late and rather elegant dinners was entirely at the bidding of Geoffrey, and a chore to Enid Faber. Later, Ann, the only one who was interested in publishing, would never be offered more than dogsbody work in the firm, which hung hopefully on to the name 'Faber and Faber' for many years, while the sons both scorned publishing and reached distinction in other arenas.

Ann was the only one of my friends who visited me at home. She was the one before whom my mother put on a bitterly shaming temper display. She came another time, a couple of years later, and we had a remarkable walking holiday together, just the two of us, staying at a Bed and Breakfast right out on Dartmoor, near Dartmeet, and exploring the moor together. It rained almost every day, but in those days the English took little notice of the weather – and all those wet walks at school had been good conditioning. Our enjoyment was undiminished.

Every day provided its own adventure. One day, we managed to get into a new-built empty house high on the hillside. Another time we came out by mistake with no money, managed to dig one shilling and sixpence, the price of one tea, out of the lining of my jacket, and talked a pub owner into allowing us to share a pot of tea, some bread and butter,

On one of our all-day holidays at Downe House

and one slice of cake. On the wettest day of all we walked a long way and dropped in without warning on my godmother, whom I had not sought out since my confirmation, at her cosy stone house outside the tiny village of Postbridge. She and her housekeeper not only made us welcome but quickly baked some scones, and tried to dry off the worst of our dripping clothes.

With the school certificate behind us, our education really began. Downe did not offer a programme for further public examinations, such as Higher School Certificate, but students aiming for university were prepared for college entrance in their chosen fields. Jean Rowntree continued to teach history to the whole class, which also benefited from a class led by her, based on the expected college entrance 'general paper'. For this, she had us write a short reasoned essay weekly on an assigned topic, usually a question of current interest or controversy, which would then be the focus of the next week's discussion. We were being taught to think, not what to think.

Jean was one of three outstanding teachers, who were also close friends; the other two were Mamie Poore, who taught English, and Ben Sanderson, who taught economics, economic history, and occasionally Latin (and who would later be the Principal of Badminton School). Ironically, just as my brothers suffered from the loss of the generation of men who would have been their teachers, and from the Post Traumatic Stress Disorder (PTSD) of those who had come through the First World War, we may have benefited from the availability of splendid single women.

In the senior forms, and out of class, we came to know Jean Rowntree well. Teachers were extraordinarily generous with their time, and we had many opportunities to benefit. The History Club was divided into sections, each doing what was, in effect, original research: one group looking into the murder of Sir Edmond Berry Godfrey, one into the origins of a number of tombs of crusading knights, and another into methods and sites of archaeological interest. I belonged to this last, and still remember the excitement of finding ancient oyster shells at an unremarkable and undug shallow ring of stones on the top of a hill, well inland, and learning that the Romans' relish for this delicacy was proof that this was indeed a Roman site. We traced on a map the route by which the oysters may have travelled, arriving fresh so far from the sea. In another remarkable exercise, we were all given a barebones account of a supposed colonial incident, and worked in small groups to write it up as it might have appeared in a wide spectrum of newspapers, including the *Times,* the *Frankfurter Zeitung* or the *Daily Worker.*

The three teacher friends also had a cosy hut in the woods around the school, and we were often made welcome there, two or three at a time, to sit around the fire and chat. What a gift to adolescents in those troubled times. Every second week, Jean lectured to the whole school on current affairs. In 1938 and 1939, this was heavy stuff.

CHAPTER 7

Light and Shade

The shadow of the coming conflict fell across our lives, particularly palpable from the time of the Munich crisis in September 1938. During that particular episode I happened to be in London, escorted by my mother, writing the London matriculation exam. The exam was held in a huge echoing hall filled with rows of desks. So close was the fear of war that I jumped when a door was slammed, half-thinking that the bombing was beginning.

Yet, in one of the strange anomalies of that time of light and dark, the year, 1939, that would see the end of attempts at peace, began for me with an unexpected skiing holiday in Switzerland with my parents. I had had to repeat an exam, which had led to my having to spend much of the Christmas holidays studying, which offended my father's commitment to leisure time for the young. So he held me back from the normal beginning of term and the three of us went off together. We flew from London – a big adventure in itself – leaving in weather that was so stormy that we nearly didn't go. I remember George seeing us off in the rain from the little Croydon airport. Planes were not pressurised then and

my ears were seriously painful when we went high to get above the storm, and also above the Alps, where it was also very bumpy. It was in fact the first and last time that I was ever motion sick. I wasn't very scared, because, never having flown before, I thought that was what it was always like. As it turns out, I have never experienced such turbulence since, not even in small planes during the war.

It was not the best time of year to be a young person on the Swiss slopes – since others of my age were all where they ought to be, in classrooms – but it was wonderful for me, both because of the skiing and because I felt a closeness to, and almost approval from, my parents, who generously rejoiced in

Harold at Wengen, January 1939

94

my ability and freedom to go farther and faster than they were able to. I have wondered since whether part of my father's thinking was to squeeze in for me some tiny part of the experience that would have been mine had the war not come. My mother took to skating (which she had done in Scotland as a youngster) and my father's skiing did not progress very far because he couldn't make his legs do the things needed to stop safely – the lower hills were quite icy, because there was not much fresh snow – and, as a surgeon, he was very cautious about any danger of damaging his hands.

Every day my skiing class took us farther afield, and on the last day we made what seemed to me a major trip, quite a long way up by train to Eigergletscher, and spent the whole day skiing down over what I remember as fresh deep snow, and with few others around. I had to leave the group somewhere near the end and ski on ahead because I was afraid I would cause us all to miss our train. I got down just in time – my mother had my travelling clothes all ready for me, and something for me to eat, and we just caught the train to Zurich to fly home. I am not sure how well I remember the details of the day, but I can still capture the sense of what was for me a big adventure.

Back at school, I found that Miss Willis had decided that, now that war was inevitable, we should be prepared for it as best we could be. Acknowledging that our lives would probably not follow the comfortable course that would earlier have been predicted, she provided opportunities for us to learn something 'useful'. Every class would take one week in the term out of the classroom and work in the kitchen. Every individual would also find or be assigned to a practical task in which she would learn a skill. I could have benefited from the kitchen experience; unfortunately those of us studying for college entrance were not allowed to participate. Nor were we expected to take part in the more time-consuming new jobs. We could not join those who rose early to milk cows, or those who helped in the school vegetable garden. But we must do something, and we were urged to think of an appropriate learning experience. Finally, Virginia and Ann and I decided that we wanted to learn about car engines. I am sure the suggestion came from me, I am not sure how much it appealed to the other two. But it was something I had wanted for a long time, especially since my brother George had bought an old Baby Austin for five pounds and spent a summer making it work again (my role in this enterprise had been limited to constantly pushing from behind to get it started). Our suggestion was accepted without argument, arrangements were made for us to spend sports time once a week at the local service station, and Miss Dorothy, a housekeeping sister of Miss Willis, bought dungarees for all of us – this novel garb in itself was quite revolutionary. One of the staff expressed nervousness at the thought that her car might be exposed to our ministrations, and another some surprise that we were to be tutored by the young mechanic. I don't think we learnt much, but we enjoyed it – not a common experience for most girls at their sheltered boarding schools.

We were all also exposed to First Aid courses, and – much more grim – to courses on poison gas. Memories of the horrors of the First World War battlefields were still fresh in the minds of the older generation, together with the knowledge that this time the war would come to us, not be fought only on the battlefields. For me the most nightmarish element was the honesty of the gas course. It was clear that all we were being taught to do was make the best of what would be a ghastly situation. There was no real protection against a poison gas attack. In retrospect, I suppose that this was in part what saved us from ever experiencing it, since both sides in that war knew retaliation was certain. We did not know then of the Nazis' ghastly use of poison gas in the concentration camps. But my own imagination was vivid enough that when war came I readily obeyed the government order to carry a gas mask at all times, and did not follow the fairly common practice among young women of removing the mask and using the case as a handy shoulder bag for my makeup. Sadly, more than sixty years later, poison gas is still used – just not against those with the capacity to retaliate.

At home, too, we spoke realistically of the probability of war. My parents had recovered from an embarrassing attraction to Nazi Germany in the early thirties. This had been brought on by a friendship with a German family who had come to England on holiday, and unexpectedly had to avail themselves of my father's professional services when the wife developed appendicitis. On a visit to Germany, they had seen only the good aspects ('the trains ran on time'), although my mother was clear that the subservient domestic position of the wife was not to her taste. And in early 1939, my father had an air raid shelter built in our garden.

At school, we, as teenagers, may well have been more knowledgeable and more emotionally engaged in the horror that was unfolding than even the average adult Briton. One of the few ways in which a citizen could help was to sponsor a refugee with private funds. Miss Willis sponsored a number, several of whom came as students, others as extra members of our school community, where, whenever possible, work was found for them, anything from teaching to gardening. One, a gentle distinguished professor who still bore the visible scars of his First-World-War service in the German army, gave a series of lectures in sociology.

Meanwhile, Jean Rowntree became more and more central in our lives. She came from the Quaker chocolate family, and had independent means, which enabled her to come and go at her own volition (and she had a red MG sports car that was for us the epitome of glamour). She and her close friend Ben Sanderson devoted their holidays to rescuing Jews from the advancing Nazi regime in Europe. As the situation worsened, she took one whole term off for this work. Inevitably, we asked her about Quakerism, and wrestled with the concept of pacifism, against a background of failed disarmament, fascist aggression, the Spanish Civil War, appeasement and a climate that had turned the vision of the 'Great' War as a war to end war (on which I had been reared) into nothing but a bitter irony. Jean herself, intimately engaging with the evils of the Nazi move to exterminate the Jews, told us that she could no longer be a complete pacifist. She had seen evil and it had to be stopped, by force if necessary. Appeasement became anathema to her. But she welcomed our struggles to think our own way through the issue.

Jean was the first Quaker I ever knew. Gradually I formed a picture of what Quakers lived by, of the role of the Inner Light. Every now and then, something she said would speak directly to me. For instance, it was a relief to learn that Friends (the alternative term for Quakers) were not expected to believe anything that was contrary to reason. I eased up on my efforts to 'believe' that the wine and wafers of communion were somehow the blood and body of Jesus. Although I liked the idea that Quakers had no creed, it was not until later that I recognised the extent to which worship could be independent of doctrine and intellectual concepts. Confirmation classes had put a lot of emphasis on the sacraments. It was a challenge to come to terms with the Quaker idea that there was no need for special ceremonies and times. Every meal and every day could be treated as a gift and an occasion for worship. Once, in the time she set aside every term to meet with each student separately, I told Olive Willis that I was drawn to Quaker ideas. Once again she proved her remarkable generosity and width of vision, reacting only with interest, and commenting that perhaps Quakerism was the most sacramental of all religions. Sometimes I attended the Quaker Meeting in Plymouth when I was home on holiday.

For me, peace had one last backhanded gift to bring before the lights went out. Early in the summer term of 1939, several of us were standing around casually engaged in the unusual occupation of actually reading what was pinned on a notice board. A small blue and white leaflet caught our attention, the notice of a coming League of Nations Union summer school for high school students, to be held in Geneva in August. Suddenly it seemed like a doable adventure. Although our school did not actively participate in the League of Nations educational programme, we were well-versed in current events, somewhat familiar with what was happening in the failing League of Nations, and attracted by the thought of Geneva, by the interesting lectures promised, and by the prospect of discussion with our peers. The cost was reasonable. About half a dozen of us wrote off to our parents, not too hopefully, to ask them to let us go. Ann's father refused outright, Felicity's parents agreed, my father embarrassed me by writing to find out if there would be a lock on my bedroom door, but, remarkably, four or five of us were allowed to register, and also signed on for a further short holiday to follow. Surely our parents must have believed that Munich really had brought 'peace in our time' to let us travel at such a time.

Late in our long summer holidays we met up in London. The adventure began with the journey across the Channel and a few hours in Paris, exploring small art shops and galleries found with the prior advice of well-travelled Jean Rowntree and her friends, who were almost as excited on our behalf as we were ourselves. Next came the second-class rail journey across Europe, overnight. Small and flexible, I slept well in a full-length resting place on the luggage rack.

The school lasted ten days. The students were all British boys and girls. A lot of planning had gone into the programme, which brought us lectures by well-grounded speakers, many of them distinguished in their fields. Norman Angell spoke on the hope of peace, a Nazi defended his beliefs, Sir Kenneth Clark (already well known, later noted for his television series, *Civilisation*) introduced us to the art exhibition from the Madrid Prado, currently taking refuge in Geneva from the Spanish Civil War; others spoke on the League of Nations, and on the history of peace and war. We visited the International Labour Organisation. Perhaps some of us also visited the home of the Women's International League for Peace and Freedom. When this organisation became the focus of my research many years later, I tried so hard to reach a vague memory I have that I almost made concrete a will o'the wisp recollection of a girls-only visit for tea to the tall building where they were centred from 1919 to 1969.

Major sessions were held in the Great Hall of the League of Nations building, the Palais des Nations. Back at the school, we were assigned to small discussion groups, care being taken to separate students from the same school. After a few days, comparing notes of our experience, we found that not only were those of us from Downe the only girls who asked a question after a lecture in the Great Hall, we were, more remarkably, the only girls who were speaking up in the discussion groups, where three of the four of us were playing a lively role. This discovery has gone far to convince me that there is no educational substitute for the type of free and open discussion we had at Downe, and for setting a climate by pattern and practice, as well as by precept. Students with us in Geneva were from co-ed as well as from male and female single-sex schools. It was depressing to realise how all-pervasive was the subtle indoctrination of women to know their place and leave the floor to men. I hope it helped us see how fortunate we were in our Downe education, but we were teenagers, and I think it as likely that it only boosted our sense of superiority.

Out of class activities included a lake trip to the Chateau de Chillon, a visit to the Prado exhibition and a scramble up Mont Salève. The last two had consequences for some of us. Felicity and I and a young man known to us only by his surname, Hawkins (bizarre to me now, but routine then), spent a great deal of our ample free time returning again and again to the Prado exhibition, becoming familiar in particular with the work of

Chateau de Chillon (postcard), August 1939

Velasquez and El Greco, discussing, buying postcards to take home, getting to know the work of two artists in depth in a way that, for me, would not come again. I fell in love with both art and Hawkins. Like all the young men I ever met when I hung out with Felicity, he fell in love with her. In those days it was called 'It'. Felicity had 'It'. I didn't. Hawkins – we discovered his first name was Lawrence – was special. But neither of us ever saw him again.

The Mont Salève outing persuaded Felicity and me to change our registration from the less adventurous post summer school stay in a hostel to a more challenging walking tour in the Alps. Curiously, we had to track down Miss Willis, on holiday in Italy, and send her a cable to gain her approval for the change. She telegraphed her blessing, but also indicated that she thought it absurd that we should have to seek it.

I already had the latest rucksack, bought in London on the recommendation of Jean Rowntree (whose qualifications as an exciting role model included extensive mountain-climbing experience), and I now added splendid mountain boots, hoping that my father would approve their reasonable price. He had given me enough money for modest spending and to cover emergencies, but disliked any suggestion of lavish purchases. The boots were good and served me for many years.

No one could quarrel with the cost of the trip itself. At the outset, the dozen of us who were going each handed over twelve shillings, just over half of £1, to cover food, lodging and transportation. Our leaders and chaperones were two male teachers and a female teacher, dedicated to seeing that we had a good experience, and – amongst other things – skilled in getting a good bargain. At the end of our week's walking trip they returned two shillings to each of us. This astounding bargain was, I think, aided by a prevailing European view that all young people should be out there walking in the mountains. Group rates were available everywhere.

Felicity and I were appointed official recorders, and kept a 'Trekkers' Log' of the trip. Felicity's family recently found a copy of this document for me. We had faithfully recorded our route, and with the aid of the journal, my daughter, Mary, and I followed the whole trip with Google maps and satellite views, a nostalgic experience for me. My memories were still vivid, but were enhanced by rereading the journal. My account here will involve many quotes from the log, with its mix of descriptions of the scenery and its very teenaged accounts of interactions with each other.

We started off from Geneva Eaux-Vives by train in the afternoon of August 12, and made our way to Sixt, changing at Annemasse into a train that seemed to us 'very French; it ran along by the side of the road and, at intervals, squeaked and hooted with excitement.' We walked to Salvagny and settled into 'two sumptuous barns'. After a delicious supper, 'we went up to a lovely waterfall about twenty minutes' walk away, where we were drenched with spray, and where we were first introduced to Mr. Evans' celebrated animal imitations. We got back at about 9:30, and after partially successful efforts at washing in the trough in the middle of the village street, we went to bed, swathed in blankets on nests of straw.'

Next morning we rose early, admired the boys' ablutions – they got right into the cold village trough – enjoyed a good breakfast, and set off up a steep path towards the Col d'Anterne. We rested during the middle of the day, and bathed in a small, cold mountain lake that we had entirely to ourselves. We recorded that one of us, Clara, 'very wisely refused to be done out of her bathe by the fact that she had no bathing dress; she bathed instead in her knickers and vest … and her glasses'. We were fortunate in our adult leaders, who were relaxed and open-minded, encouraging us to move way beyond our previous experience. What comes through in my memories is that they did a good job of setting us free from the proprieties and inhibitions we were ordinarily so bound by. Our first mishap occurred when Miss Feaver, our chaperone, was bitten so badly by a vicious deerfly that she was unable to get her boot back on, and had to leave the expedition for several days.

We started off again mid-afternoon, and reaching the top of the Col d'Anterne pass, 'had, for a few seconds, the most wonderful view of the top of Mont Blanc' before it was hidden by clouds. When the clouds persisted, we went on down to what seemed to us 'the rather dilapidated chalet known as the Hotel du Col d'Anterne', where considerable bargaining was necessary to secure a good price. 'After supper … when we finally dispelled the illusion that we were a quiet set of people, we went on up the hillside and saw a heavenly sunset, which lit up Mont Blanc and the other peaks with a lovely pink colour (words as usual being completely inadequate). We watched the sun go down and the colour fade', before going back to the hotel. Here our accommodation was just below the roof, in straw-filled spaces of unassigned occupancy – late arriving strangers, male and female, moved in during the night wherever they could find space (so much for my father's anxiety for a door with a lock in Geneva).

The daily routine was to take whatever breakfast was available where we stayed, and wherever possible, to eat a good plain supper at the next lodging place. We carried lunch with us. Remembering the casual sleeping arrangements horrifies me not at all, but I do have some doubts about the vast open tin of paté carried, unrefrigerated, by one of our leaders throughout the trip and spread by us daily on delicious bread (usually fresh). We also ate chocolate with our bread, from those big characteristic bars produced by an alpine people that had the good sense to recognise chocolate as a regular food, not just an occasional treat. The log, informed by teenage appetites, pays a good deal of attention to food – quantity even more than content – and also, more surprisingly, to what facilities there were for our ablutions.

Next day we made our way over the Brévent Pass to Chamonix. I have warm memories of hiking along in single file behind Mr. Nicol, who had a good repertoire of Scottish songs. The 'Road to the Isles' is still a favourite for me. Something else new came to me from him. I had occasionally met people who routinely went to the Highlands for the deer hunting season: now I met and understood a man who saw this as nothing but the exercise of colonial privilege, and who spoke hotly of his own personal resistance to the privatisation of hillsides that should have been public. We ate our lunch in a hot, dense mist before going on down to Chamonix, two, who had blisters, going on by téléférique, and the rest of us, walkers, 'having … a very hot journey down'. Mr. Evans left us in Chamonix, Miss Feaver rejoined us, we shopped for provisions, and we set out for another hot walk, this time uphill to Montenvers, high up on the mountainside. When we reached the hotel, we were directed to a room set aside for walking parties, and found ourselves 'in the lap of luxury as there were beds … we were all together in a large dormitory and with skilful organisation we made nine beds fit thirteen people', all the males being in one composite bed, all the females in another. Finding a ladies washroom with hot and cold running water was a delight and I recall that we rather took it over, although I fancy that it was intended for the use of the hotel guests, not for such as us.

Mer de Glace

The next day was long, and full of new experiences. We started off very early. The hotel provided us with a good breakfast before we left – even though that was at 4:30 am.

102

*Climbing up from the
Mer de Glace*

We were soon on the Mer de Glace, and made our way across it following a guide hired for the day. 'When we left the glacier we went up quite a steep rock chimney. A photograph in which the iron rail and the steps were cut out would be quite impressive. We reached the Couvercle hut at about 8.30 and had brunch there. We had watched the dawn on the way up and by brunch-time it was pretty warm. We separated and had until 11.30 to do as we liked.'

My recent Google observations confirm that the Couvercle hut is still there, a bit larger than I remember it as being, but the Leschaux glacier is hard to find. In 1939 it was massive and within a few metres of the Hut, 'a very superior sort of glacier with tremendous crevasses, turquoise blue in colour, about 50-60 feet deep. Morgan [a fellow trekker] armed with an ice axe, conducted a very select party which even went down one crevasse intentionally and nearly went down several others.' The beauty of the glacier is still vivid in my mind.

From the sublime to the ridiculousness of teenagers. The journal continues: 'After lunch in the hut we set off and as the guide was in a tearing hurry and evidently had a date at the bottom we came down rather fast. As we were clambering down the Leschaux glacier Lampard (one of us) sprained his ankle, but even this did not make any noticeable difference to the guide's pace. We … decided it was ludicrous to rush like that when we had the whole afternoon before us, so we determinedly slowed down. When we were some distance behind the guide, Janet, thinking he was rather lonely, shoved by everyone else to the danger of all lives and limbs except her own (she

Outside the Ski Club Hut

103

was on the inside of the narrow path) and joined him, ostensibly for the purpose of practising her French. A great deal of slander was the result of this episode.' A lazy evening writing postcards, another good meal and an early sleep (in our nine beds) brought our time at Montenvers to an end. The next day we walked along a ridge above Chamonix, and through a larch wood, but were unable to cross the Bossuet glacier without a guide, so we made our way down to the valley 'and walked along hot white dusty roads to the station which seemed to get farther and farther away', arriving just ten minutes before our train was due. During that ten minutes, 'someone bought a *Paris-Soir* and we were reminded with a horrible bump of Hitler and Danzig'. Suddenly, the shadows were closing in.

We still had a day or two. We were headed for Mont Joly, via St Gervais, and had the pleasure of a téléférique ride halfway up the mountain, where we spent a night in the Tagui ski hut, courtesy of the Geneva Ski Club (arranged, I think, by Mr. Evans). 'It was by far the most luxurious quarters we had. The dortoirs were large and airy and there were three blankets apiece. The dining room had been newly decorated and there was a lovely smell of wood which permeated everything … For supper we went to Chez Rémy, where we had a very rowdy and satisfying meal.'

The next day we climbed to the top of Mont Joly. 'We set off by seven. As it was rather late it soon began to get really hot, and we staggered slowly up the ridge. When we arrived at a little chalet at the bottom of Mont Joly some of us had cups of delicious cold milk and all of us ate

Mont Joly

some fruit and chocolate. We left our rucksacks there and climbed the rest of the way unburdened. The view from the top of Mont Joly was glorious in spite of some misty clouds which threatened to surround us. We could see the Italian Alps in one direction, to Mont Blanc in another, to the Mont Fleury range in another.'

Little remained of our trip except a steep walk down, a last picnic 'where we had a successful attempt to finish up the remaining food'. And a bus trip back to Geneva: 'the bus was full but we bought up all the back seats and sat in two layers. We were so economical with the space we had that we managed to pile some friendly Americans in as well. All the way we sang, going over our repertoire again and adding some new ones.' In Geneva, 'our boots felt and sounded most odd as we walked on the pavements to the Rigot [the school where we had accommodation], feeling that we could walk to the moon … The next day (we) left for England, the crisis and worse'.

Rightly or not, I have focused this account mainly on the journey itself, with the wonders that were so new to me. I have not attempted to paint thumbnail sketches of my fellow trekkers, and have left out many tales of the teenage interactions, the tussling in the dust at the top of Mont Joly, the attempts to deprive Morgan of his beloved beret, or to find the most suitable nickname for Renwick. I can give only a brief note about a very few of my companions. Felicity and I remained friends to the end of her life. A boy named Renwick, much smitten with her, remained in touch for quite a while. Morgan and Joan both came up to Oxford, he to Magdalen, Joan to Somerville (with me); a year or two later, they married. He was killed in Europe. I met Joan again some fifty years later at a Somerville reunion.

The summer school experience in Geneva was the biggest thing that had happened to me, putting me out into a new world of independent thought and interaction, halfway to adulthood, with new freedoms, new promise, and new challenges. The world we studied was deeply troubled, but we were young and surely we would have the chance to put it right. We knew too much of evil, by report, but we had put our faith in ourselves and the many people of goodwill whom we knew.

We came down from the mountains to find that appeasement, inevitably (and this time surely appropriately) had failed again, and we went home knowing, as we had known all along in our heads but not our hearts, that our hopes and dreams had been foolishness. Yet we had surely been changed by our experiences in Geneva and the Alps and had them stored somewhere to carry into the darkness with us.

CHAPTER 8

Last School Term

My childhood ended on September 3rd, 1939, when war was declared. The long summer holiday was nearing its end, so I was still at home. That morning, I went to the Quaker Meeting, knowing that by the time it was over, we would be at war. I had still one term at school to go. For me, the coming of the war was huge. During those first months of the war, it was quite common to hear someone say, 'Oh, I forgot there was a war on!' I cannot say why, but I never forgot. Throughout the long six years the war weighed heavily on me.

School was a good place to be for that first term of the war, although there were already changes to get used to. Virginia had been whisked off to South Africa – not unexpectedly – by her mother. Two months later, we received a vivid account of her long, slow voyage in a small cargo vessel, with her mother and four fervent German Nazi supporters as the only other passengers. Felicity, who now ranked as one of my closest friends, had not come back to school. Meanwhile, Ann Faber's parents may have regretted not allowing her to come to Geneva with us. She had instead spent that last desperate summer before the war developing an intense relationship, and came back to school unofficially engaged, against the wishes of her parents. Alan, her fiancé, was due to be called to the army almost immediately. I, so profoundly unlearned in the world of dating and mating which we were all entering, was nevertheless seen by Ann's mother as a steadying influence. This view was sufficiently shared by Miss Willis that, although we were both senior students, we were put together in a corridor that was my responsibility, rather than each having our own separate areas. We shared a coveted double room – most rooms were for three, four or six students. Ann's family and to some extent our teachers at school thought her immature; perhaps she was, but she may have been made more so by their attitude. Like me, she was a senior; unlike me, she had no responsibilities – and of all the dozy teenagers who were my responsibility, I found her the hardest to get out of bed in the morning; an unhappy youngster moving into adulthood.

We returned to school to find that we were playing host to another school, evacuated from London. I am embarrassed when I recall the enormous sense we had of the superiority of our school over all others, but there is some comfort in the recognition that class was not the issue. They were far more class-conscious than we were. But, much as I hate to

Olive Willis with Senior girls, 1939. On the left, Virginia is at the back,
Jo in the middle row, and Ann Faber in the front. Felicity is on Miss Willis's left

think it, I now suspect indeed that the arrangement had been made with our socially acceptable visitors in order to stave off a less-than-voluntary invasion by a state school or institution. Elitism was not absent from Miss Willis's thinking, however much she instilled in us the idea of courtesy and kindness to all.

Miss Spalding's school was akin to a 'finishing school' for very proper and well-to-do young ladies. Our school was outdoorsy, rural in location, musical, serious in discussions, and inclined towards high achievement in scholarship and sports. I and my friends (except now, Ann) – who I now see were not necessarily representative of the whole school – were not, during term time, particularly interested in boys or our appearance and certainly not in our marriage prospects. Without bothering to find much out about Miss Spalding's girls, we simply settled for despising them. For good or ill, Miss Willis had seen to it that we mingled as little as possible.

My only direct encounter with Miss Spalding came on an evening when a couple of us were out for a stroll after dark. We were asked by a passing Air Raid Warden to draw Miss Spalding's attention to a gap in the blackout curtain at a house on the grounds, which our guest school occupied. Somewhat officiously, we were glad to do this. The response we received was anything but friendly. The door was answered by Miss Spalding herself, but she was not interested in our message. Shocked that we were out unsupervised, she attacked our credibility, implied doubt of the existence of the Warden, and inferred that if we had met someone it had probably been by assignation. We left reeling, but secretly rather pleased than otherwise to be able to put some substance behind our distaste for our visitors. We told Miss Willis, whose concern, rightly, was mainly to make sure that the blackout was indeed adequate.

During that, my last term at Downe, I benefited more than ever from the opportunities for discussion, from the continuing reassuring routine, from the closeness of the senior girls to Jean Rowntree and, yes, to Olive Willis. Yet I could not wait to be out in the world – though I had very little idea what I would be able to do out there, now that the hope of spending part of my gap year abroad had gone.

Some time during that last term we sat our college entrance exams. Qualification for admission to the university, in prewar days, came from achieving the appropriate credits on the school certificate or London matriculation exams. For most young men then, an interview and the willingness and ability of their fathers to pay the fees would get them into one or other college. I am not familiar with the further subtleties of elitism or specific public school background that determined which college. From my perspective, it seemed that there were plenty of men's colleges to accommodate all paying comers, whether they were there to learn or simply to pass the time, and to walk away – it was hoped – with a pass degree.

For women, the position was different. At Oxford there were four women's colleges with a limited number of places. The colleges would only take women who could be expected to take an honours degree. We had to compete for a place through the college entrance exam. Although this seemed to us a big and important hurdle to jump, it was insignificant indeed compared with the present day. The really worthy among those admitted were the handful of scholarship students who had had to confront opposition from all sides and compete at every level of a system not designed to lead to a post-secondary education. The rest of us had had all the privileges of private schools and private tutoring, and a sort of self-selection – even at my school, probably only about one third of us aimed to continue our education. In my hometown, only one girl of my cohort, the children of professionals, was known to me to be university-bound. My Plymouth tennis-playing acquaintances thought me pretty odd. My father's ungrudging commitment to funding equal educational opportunities for me with my brothers was exceptional.

When the college exam results came out (after I had returned home) I was relieved that I had obtained a place, and not, perhaps, very surprised that it was contingent on my improving my Latin, which had always been a bugbear to me. There was no celebration. I don't think my parents had ever realised that this was an exam in which one could fail.

Virginia was only one among a considerable number of students who had not returned because of the war, and the number included one or two who would have been in line to serve as Head Senior. Towards the end of the term, Olive Willis called me in, and asked me to stay on another term, and fill this position, an honour and an opportunity. I had my mind ready to leave, despite the uncertainties, and I turned down the offer. I did not tell her, and I have told scarcely anyone since, but the real reason was that I was overwhelmed by the thought of the responsibility involved. Many years later, when I read the work of the psychologist R. D. Laing, I recognised a precise description of what I had experienced. He describes what I felt: a sense of panic in the face of expectations, a fear of being found out, a sense that I would never be able successfully to hide from people the fact that I was not as good, as efficient, as able as they thought I was. I knew that Miss Willis's expectations were based on her observations and on my performance as repeatedly elected class leader – my classmates had even done me the great honour of making sure that I would be available for the crucial half term of our major public exams – but, in my mind, that had all been a sham, too. By some fluke I had never let my classmates down, yet, I was certain, this had not been because of any real competence, just some ability to hide my incompetence. So I refused the challenge, telling Miss Willis that I could not change my mind about leaving. What I lost was a term of working closely with Miss Willis as my mentor, an opportunity that could have benefited me in many ways. It might also have been good for me to discover that I really was able to do the job.

It would be many, many years before the sense of unrevealed but profound inadequacy completely passed from me, and I am sure it cost me other opportunities. And yet, as my stories will show, I was capable of showing confidence in my own judgement – sometimes more than was warranted.

CHAPTER 9

After School:
Yorkshire and Mount View

When I left school in December 1939, a long year stretched ahead, full of the unpredictable threats of war – which, so far, had not hit us hard – and with no clear plans in my own suddenly insignificant life. I had no particular obligations, except to work for a few hours a week at that wretched Latin, until it would be time to go up to Oxford in the autumn. What had been planned as a gap year spent in Europe turned into a gap year of new experiences.

Our lives were much changed by the need to be prepared. We daily expected bombing, but for the first few months air raids were few and consisted only of a single plane coming over, usually on reconnaissance. My mother had volunteered with the St. John Ambulance Service, Nannie undertook a weekly shift at the local air raid post and the nearby school became a temporary mess for young, newly recruited medical officers. Douglas, newly qualified as a doctor, was interning in London, my father worked harder than ever and George, enjoying his one permitted year at Cambridge before conscription, came home from time to time to lighten the atmosphere. We still went to dances, usually at the Moorland Links Hotel outside the city. Gradually our tennis-playing friends disappeared into the navy, army or marines.

My closest friends had left school with me and we kept in touch with letters. We also wrote with restrained desperation to our beloved mentor, Jean Rowntree, who replied faithfully, always taking us seriously. From her, early in January 1940, came news of a nursery school evacuated from York to the deep countryside and in need of volunteer help. Felicity planned to go, and I was determined to join her. We understood that the children would be housed in a big old empty country house, and that the volunteers lived quite basically in a nearby cottage. My father was not impressed with the sound of it, especially as we volunteers had to contribute a weekly ten shillings each to cover the cost of our food. I don't remember any other time when a small cost bothered my father, but it irked him to have to put out money to have me go away (when he would rather have me at home) to do volunteer work with children (when there was plenty of that to be done in Plymouth) and live in discomfort (when I could perfectly well live comfortably at home). To my

*The cottage we lived in was one of a row of three, rumoured to have been condemned
25 years earlier, and not lived in since.*

embarrassment, he insisted on speaking directly by telephone to Jean
Rowntree, who told him that, yes, the work we were wanted for was
menial; and yes, we would have to do our own cooking; and yes, the
cottage we would live in had no running water, no toilet other than pails
in a shed out back, no telephone and no electricity. When he put the
phone down, and repeated all this information to me, he clearly thought
his point was made. Bless him, with his usual generosity, he gave in with
good grace as soon as it was clear that I was as keen as ever to go.

Felicity and I spent two months at the nursery school, which, in
retrospect, was a rather ill-thought-out project. In those early days of the
war, a consuming impulse for many people was to remove the children
from any city where bombing might be expected. The nucleus of those
we were charged with, gathered together in the big house, was a York day
nursery. To this had been added an orphanage and then, for good
measure, an assortment of children from homes deemed 'unsatisfactory'
by social workers. The threat of bombing was a good pretext. Few people
thought the wholesale removal of children was a rash experiment. In
York it was less comprehensive than the mass removal from London, but
nonetheless disruptive. The Quakers contributed to the effort (hence Jean
Rowntree's connection, and ours), which now I see as one of their less
inspired social moves. In the event, York was scarcely bombed.

A number of young Quakers had helped out at the school during the early days of the war and had moved on to other things by the time winter fell. Felicity and I found ourselves alone in our little cottage, with the adjoining one occupied by a married couple we saw as grown up, but who I now realise were very little older than ourselves. John was a conscientious objector assigned to farm work. He worked hard and was paid at a less-than-living rate by the farmer, who was also supposed to supply them with some produce. They seldom saw the scarce eggs or occasional chicken to which they were entitled – and certainly not if the farmer could find someone who would pay good money for them. Cathy was pregnant and had wisely discontinued her earlier role as chief housekeeper to the assorted young volunteers. She continued to help us out with occasional much-needed advice.

Cathy also brought us our weekly groceries. I am still almost embarrassed to confess that our education had been so lacking regarding the essentials of living that we hardly knew what to ask for or what to do with it when we got it. Everyone, we thought, had a roast on Sunday, so we contrived to cook one, usually lamb, and ate it with potatoes and carrots. Greens were not available. Fortunately rationing had not come into force at that time, so that our roasts were large enough to eat cold on Monday and Tuesday. My mind is a blank on how we got through the rest of the week. Perhaps we had sausages, rarely eggs (we did not like to compete with Cathy for this precious commodity). We had good bread and a large stone jar of treacle – later in the year the jar was found to have a well-preserved dead mouse at the bottom, but this was after I had left.

Even these modest culinary efforts were something of a challenge. The old cast-iron kitchen range was small, and though I do not remember any shortage of coal, we had a lot of trouble getting it going, which we ascribed to our general incompetence. What had seemed to be one of its better features – a small tank of hot water at the side – proved to be in fact the culprit. It was cracked and leaking into the fire compartment. When we reluctantly relinquished this one small source of hot water, the stove worked better.

There were elements in our domestic arrangements that would have been a challenge to most people, let alone youngsters as extraordinarily ignorant as we were. Felicity and I had both been bypassed, because of academic priorities, by Miss Willis's right-minded if belated efforts to have us all serve a spell in the school kitchens. I knew how to boil water: not much more. Remember that I had seldom been in the kitchen at home, except for a brief effort initiated by myself, when I was about thirteen, to have the cook teach me how to make breakfast. I would have known how to scramble eggs, if we had had any. The experience of making fudge with Nannie on the nursery gas ring was singularly irrelevant. But we survived, and surprisingly, we continued to enjoy each other's company.

The school housed forty children and was staffed during regular daytime hours by two reluctant primary teachers who had been assigned the job, apparently against their wishes. Then there were two daycare trainees, two local girls and the two of us. The whole was overseen by a matron, qualified and dedicated, skilled with the

Ann Faber volunteered later in the year. Summer was a happier time for the children

children but not at helping others develop those skills. Once, completely unable to get a child to dress for breakfast, I had to call for her help; one look from her and Johnny was clothed – another look and I was crushed.

We dressed the children in the morning and again after their noon rest, and we and the village girls bathed them in back-breaking old baths in the evening – a lovely time as they were relaxed and chatty at that time of day. We cleaned and polished the many oil lamps that supplemented the small home-generated supply of electricity. We helped the local washerwoman with the weekly mountain of laundry. The children ranged in age from two to five years; homesick and with little encouragement towards toilet training, many of them wet their pants (or worse) and their small cots every night, some again during the noon rest.

No attempt was made to keep the clothing of individual children separate – each child was clothed in whatever came to hand. As for the washing, we – as ignorant about laundry as we were about cooking – did what the washerwoman told us, working in a cobbled building in the yard, standing on a damp floor, working between an icy draft and a blazing fire which melted soap, dried the clothes and heated the irons. I contracted chilblains for the first and last time in my life. The 'washing

113

George Street, Plymouth, before the war

machine' consisted of a hand-operated pivoted board in a wooden sink. Rinsing was usually skipped and sometimes a recognisable streak of hardened soap could be found on some garment in the clean clothes cupboard. It has occurred to me since that we could have had a better tutor than that particular washerwoman.

What this life was like for the children is hard now to imagine. Growing up ourselves in a sub-culture where it was commonplace to send children to boarding school quite early, and where – certainly in my case – cuddling was seen as a rather weak indulgence, we were less aware than we might have been that the children's lives lacked an essential ingredient. Looking back, I see the village girls as having had the healthiest attitude. True, they had favourites, a practice righteously abhorred by Felicity and me, but they treated the children with spontaneous affection, as they might have their own small siblings, somehow conveying to some, for at least a few minutes here and there, that feeling of being loved and special that all children need.

We felt at times a real depth of love, but whether we conveyed it I don't know. I do remember in particular a pair of brothers. Joe was a very serious nearly-five-year-old. Jimmy his delinquent three-year-old brother, always causing trouble, always in disgrace. Joe loved him and cared about him. We would talk about the problems at bath time. Their mother, I learnt, was dead, their father away in the army. When Joe turned five he would have to go elsewhere to begin formal education – bad enough for their tiny family. And then I heard that their father had been killed. I never found out what happened to them, but – clueless eighteen-year-old as I was – I would have adopted them if I could have figured out a way.

There were many lighter moments. One afternoon, going into one of the dormitories to get the children up after their mid-day rest, I was

114

confronted by a sea of multi-coloured wool. The children slept on little canvas beds, attractively covered with small quilts made up of squares of wool, painstakingly and unevenly knitted by young and old volunteers all over the country (in the First World War, I understand, knitting socks was the thing; in the second, I am sure it must have been squares – I came across them everywhere). But this afternoon, some little demon – perhaps it was Jimmy – had discovered that if you pulled a loose end of wool, it all began to unravel entrancingly, and, if there wasn't a loose end, you could soon make one, and another, and another. Who could resist joining in?

At this time, the children were seldom outside. We were virtually snowed in almost all that winter. It was bitterly cold in our primitive cottage. Our bedding had been donated by a private school that was restocking. We had lots of blankets, but they were thinner than any others I have ever seen, so we piled them on. We had cherished hot water bottles and washed minimally in the still warm water from them in the mornings. We took it in turns to be first up and go downstairs by candlelight to start the fire.

Two boys from Bootham, a Quaker boys' school evacuated from York to the Catholic school at Downside, biked over from time to time to empty our bucket toilets. They continued their occasional visits after the buckets froze solid, finding that their volunteer work had changed into a pleasurable visit with two young women of about their own age (one of whom – guess which one – was decidedly attractive). We enjoyed the break as much as they did. Other visitors included, very rarely, Tessa Rowntree (Jean's cousin) who bore welcome gifts – treacle, or the first box of kitkat bars that I ever saw.

All of this seemed like adventure to us. I don't think we ever saw it as hardship, until a severe flu epidemic struck. Felicity was the first of us to go down, with sudden violent vomiting in the night. I cleaned up after her and must have managed to get a message to Tessa, who came and took her away to recuperate. The washerwoman failed to turn up, and, short-staffed all round, whoever was in charge left me to do the washing. I was (and still am!) proud of having single-handedly, and by hand, done all the week's laundry for forty children, that one time. I won't vouch for the standard.

At about this time, I had a misunderstanding with my brother Douglas, who was now a senior medical student working in the East End of London, and was something of a hero to me. I wrote and told him I was thinking of a career in social work. However, while I had a fairly sophisticated understanding of this as being now a regular profession, he, it seems, had only an out-of-date picture of a social worker as some kind of unqualified Lady Bountiful, patronising the ground-down women he served. He wrote to denigrate my ambition, making it clear that he thought that I had no idea what I was talking about. I was too hurt to write back and tell him of my laundry feat or explain what 'social work' meant to me.

Shortly afterwards, I too came down with flu. I have only a vague memory of this, perhaps because I was, indeed, very ill for a few days. I think Felicity must have been back by this time. When I was finally seen by a doctor, he found a slight heart murmur, and I was duly packed off home. My father still refrained from saying 'I told you so', and I have never regretted the experience I gained (nor has the heart murmur recurred).

At home, I spent the next few months doing this and that. I was obliged to study Latin, to bring it up to the satisfactory standard I had failed to reach in my Somerville College entrance exams. My father provided a succession of tutors. The first was a rather ineffectual, elderly man whom I visited in his lodgings just before lunch time and of whom I remember only the remarkable vividness of his abdominal rumblings. The second was a tough, macho, pipe-smoking schoolmaster, an effective tutor. I recall a resounding crash when his small son collided with his

St. Andrew's Church before the war

Guildhall Square, Plymouth

Before the war: Guildhall Square and St. Andrew's Church

smaller daughter, knocking her over. She screamed, clearly in some pain. Mr. Grant shifted his pipe to the other side of his mouth and commented briefly, 'She has to learn to take it'. His wife removed the children. Mr. Grant was involved in organising the Local Defence Volunteers, soon to be renamed the Home Guard, and drew me in to assist with setting up a card file of volunteers. I did not try to discuss the pacifist option with him, or indeed, with anyone else at home, but I felt slightly compromised as a putative pacifist.

I found voluntary work with pre-school children, helping out one or two days each week at a day care facility down near the Hoe. Here I was exposed to good modern methods of care, more educational for me than what I had seen in my role as dogsbody in the makeshift Yorkshire facility. Gradually, we became used to frequent air raids, initially involving single planes, but scary and disruptive. The children arrived at daycare tired and tense, but, as children will, they worked out some of the tensions by playing out the everyday occurrences of their lives. They designated a corner of the patio as the air raid shelter. A small boy named Georgie perfected the sound of the siren. Playing 'families', they would go about ordinary routines until Georgie sounded off, when they would rush to the corner. After a while Georgie sounded the All Clear, so they cautiously emerged. More often than not, they were halfway out when Georgie sounded the siren again, at which they exclaimed, 'Oh there it

117

goes again!', just as their mothers had the previous night, and dived back into the corner.

The value of this normalising game was recognised by the wise staff, and they did nothing to discourage it. But they had to make one modification: Georgie became so good at sounding the siren that we could not distinguish it from the real thing. He had to be stopped, as there, on the Hoe, we were vulnerable, and small daytime raids were also occurring. When the real siren went off, the children at first showed fear and a tendency to panic, but the staff established a pattern of quiet response, lining the children up and leading them quietly to the basement, which was, for what it was worth, our air raid shelter. Calm behaviour proved to be as infectious as panic.

I also found my way to a child care set-up that was auxiliary to a weekly prenatal and postnatal clinic presided over by Dr Thynne, a Quaker doctor whose name I knew through my continuing sporadic attendance at the Plymouth Quaker Meeting. Here Mrs. Hamley, a child psychologist from Bermuda, took care of small children while their mothers, pregnant again, attended the clinic. I soon found that Mrs. Hamley's role went far beyond keeping the children out of the way. She

Tidied up after the bombing (postcard)

was observing the children – some of whom had been specifically referred by Dr. Thynne – and identifying behavioural problems, some related to complaints the mothers had made of their unmanageability. She had a gift for suggesting small modifications in the way difficulties were handled, and was often able to make a real difference. I helped keep the children entertained. But even then I sometimes wondered whether Mrs. Hamley made me welcome less for the very modest help I gave than for the real need she perceived in me. I am sure I benefited as much as the children from her friendship, her wisdom and her gift for understanding the young. I lost touch with her when I left home,

118

Services were sometimes held here, in the open air

but many years later, when I was back in Plymouth with two small children of my own, I found my way to her in a crisis. It is hard to describe her help on that occasion as anything other than heaven-sent – she may have saved my life.

Life at Mount View had changed. We had less staff, and lived more simply. There was one near-tragic casualty of the increased pressure. The stalwart and jolly Mr. Dyer had given way as gardener to a man of a very different type. Although I can't remember his name – so I shall call him Thomas – I particularly liked this man, who lived in the cottage with his wife. He was a small man, sensitive, clearly a lover of nature and attuned – it seemed to me – to the same deep spirit that I had found to be so palpable whenever I spent time in the garden. We all liked him. My mother and I agreed that he could be described as 'fey', meaning that he had some connection to nature beyond that granted to most of us. He thought the world of my father.

Martin, the gardener's assistant, had found war work in the dockyard; Northcote spent more of his time on the cars (and like all of us, was I am sure, doing some voluntary war work). Thomas, who could not bear to let anything slip in the smallest degree, and was, I think, profoundly affected by the constant bombing, overworked himself into a breakdown, eventually, I believe, attempting suicide. His distraught wife told my mother that he had kept saying he felt he was letting my father down by his inability to get through all the work. Although I was at home at the time, I was never made privy to just what happened, though I knew there was a crisis. I hope my father, one of whose failings lay in his inability to see anything but moral weakness in any kind of emotional or mental breakdown, did not show disappointment in Thomas. In the outcome, Thomas was at least well looked after. He had previously worked on the D'Oyley Carte estate (the family which owned the performance rights to the Gilbert and Sullivan operas), perhaps had even grown up there. The D'Oyley Cartes immediately agreed to have him come back to them. I believe it was deep in the country, away from bombs. I hope he made a full recovery there, and found the work he loved in a less stressful situation.

Even before war began, Father had had an air raid shelter built, fitted with bunks to accommodate eight people. He had also had to solve the problem of how to black out the large square skylight in the centre of the house, installing a pulley-operated blind, which we had to remember to close.

My mother had also made her preparations for the war. Her old hospital – the Royal Free in Glasgow – had sent a circular to all its old graduates some months earlier, offering a short course to upgrade their skills. Oddly enough, Jo was the only one to apply, so they did not run the course they had planned. Instead they offered my mother a unique opportunity to spend time sitting in on whatever aspects of their current work she wished. Her privileges may have been based as much on my father's reputation as on her long-ago studentship. The experience was rich for her, and she made good use of it. When she came home, she volunteered with the St. John Ambulance, donned a uniform and worked with them, but with a good deal of autonomy, for the duration of the war. She was courageous and a good organiser. Perhaps she felt fulfilled for the first time for many years. Among other things, she served as liaison to the families of men from the Allied forces who were admitted to our local hospitals. In another capacity, she was authorised to request leave for men whose wives were seriously ill. On one occasion at the request of a sick woman she summoned her husband, a sergeant. Unfortunately, the husband identified on the women's papers, and summoned by the staff nurse, was not the same man my mother had summoned. When she was called to the hospital, she found the two husbands together in the waiting room. Luckily, they shared a common disgust at their wife's perfidious way of obtaining two army allowances, and did not come to blows with each other.

As spring came, the phoney war gave way rapidly to deadly serious warfare, and the Allies did not fare well. Suddenly France was falling. The rescue of much of the army from Dunkirk by the civilian fleet of small ships profoundly moved us all. Few expected the Channel to be an effective barrier for long.

Many French soldiers landed at much the same time as the Dunkirk survivors, and were sent down to Plymouth by rail to embark for what was still left of Free France. My mother was called to help them on their way with First Aid and cups of tea. But barely were the docks clear of them than the rest of France capitulated. A new flood of refugees began to arrive, while German planes bombed and strafed them, and at times the docks as well. Sometimes I joined my mother as she greeted the ill-assorted arrivals: a shipload of Breton peasants who should never have left home; scattered refugees from the Channel Islands – of these I remember most vividly two children, a young brother and sister whose parents had sent them with the promise of soon following – they were on the dock for several days, and no parents arrived. I do not know how they were cared for.

Docking space was inadequate for the need. Ships stood off the coast for several days, short of food and water and exposed to attack. Some priority was given to a ship full of mothers with small babies in desperate need of milk. George happened to be there when they arrived and was sent off to hunt for supplies. With his usual efficiency, he quickly raised needed bottles from a local orphanage and bought milk. Then there were men who had been picked up from a ship that had been sunk, some with burns from an oil fire that had spread across the water. And then, suddenly, there was my Uncle George, my mother's youngest brother, who was serving as a chaplain in the army. He too had been in the water, but was not burned.

Throughout the early summer we waited for the invasion. I never shared with anyone my particular dread on behalf of my beloved mentor, Jean Rowntree, who we, her disciples, knew was on Hitler's most wanted list. A sense of the inevitability of bad things to come was tangible. No wonder we loved Winston Churchill's oratory, challenging us to believe that we could beat the Nazis back from our shores and 'beat the buggers over the head with bottles as it's all we've got,' as I was told he had added below his breath to one of his strongest perorations. During the high summer the Battle of Britain raged over our heads. Daily we counted the scores. Even then I was shamed by the rejoicing. So many of our planes down, so many of theirs – so many young men,

German or British, dying in agony, nothing but horror and nausea when 'one of theirs' spiralled, flaming, out of control and people cheered. What a confusion of emotions: gratitude, pride, compassion, a gradual sense of relief and hope, and an overwhelming realisation that the war still had years to run.

I was, I think, closer to my parents during the war than ever before. I appreciated my mother's enterprise and her courage on the docks, and I was grateful for her ability, not easy for her, to acknowledge that my childhood was at an end. As for my father, I loved to be woken up in the night to accompany him when he was called to one of the country hospitals for an emergency. It was hard to get him to wake me, although he had always preferred to have someone with him on night calls – usually his driver (though he was only allowed to drive him home). Once, I was really of use: the fog was so thick on the moor that I had to lean out of the car to watch the side of the road, while he peered ahead intent on avoiding any stray Dartmoor ponies. And then there was the Home Guard, who were provided with inadequate lanterns and with guns (fortunately perhaps also inadequate) and might appear anywhere along a country road and challenge passing vehicles. On another occasion, we ran into extensive military movement. Perhaps there was an invasion alert. Car lights had been cut down by regulation to what was judged to be the minimum for safety: now we were ordered to turn them off altogether, and crept along for many miles by moonlight. I felt safe with my father, not perhaps physically, but deeply – spiritually may be the word. We had good talk on these night drives.

On Sundays my father attended the Anglican Church in the morning when he could, and in the evening he liked sometimes to go to one of the other Protestant denominations; occasionally I went with him. In the mornings, I quite often went to the Quaker Meeting (why, oh why, did no one there reach out to me, as they would have to a young man seeking for answers in time of conscription?). My father explained carefully that he felt unable to accompany me. He much admired the Quakers he knew, but he was prevented from coming with me because he, too well known in the city, could not be seen associating with pacifists in this time of war. He did not put down my choice, nor did he try to influence me. He accorded me an adult respect, which I valued. But I regret that pacifism itself was one of the many topics we avoided.

Wartime experiences, especially those at Mount View, had (and retain for me) a curious aura of unreality about them, the product perhaps of experiencing such uncertainty and doubt in surroundings that had been associated with almost rock-solid security.

I relate only what I experienced myself, and I don't remember the timing very exactly. Heavy raids only built up at the very end of that summer of 1940, and I shall have to return to this topic. The London blitz began in September, just before I went up to Oxford for my first term.

Chapter 10

Oxford

By the time the summer of 1940 was over, the war had begun in earnest. In September the London blitz started. My father took a couple of days off and drove me himself up to Oxford, where he settled me into my Somerville room, adding a good high-backed chair, a footstool that I still have and a couple of cushions. My 'dress' allowance would be £1 a week, paid quarterly. Later this was increased to £20 a quarter, more in line with most of my friends. Unfortunately my father later changed this again, making me responsible for paying my own fees, and giving me a lump sum of £200, with directions to ask for more when I needed it. I think the new way of doing it had something to do with tax benefits, and I suppose it showed his trust in me, but it was highly unsatisfactory, as it left me always feeling guilty whatever I spent.

I found Ann Faber already in residence. Her parents had had to evacuate their Hampstead house until the authorities had detonated an unexploded bomb in their garden, so she had been packed off early. She had already formed a group of friends, and I fell in with them comfortably. Later, I realised that another small group of first year students might have been better for me. Their interests were more in social justice issues. But I was lazy and perhaps shy and made no move towards them. The history entrants also saw a great deal of each other. There were ten of us, and we had May McKisack, a distinguished mediaevalist, as our 'moral tutor', a vague term that meant she kept a reserved eye on our individual well-being (and behaviour?) as well as a close one on our academic progress.

The Oxford curriculum – and process – was very different from anything I have experienced since. In our first term we had to polish off Pass Mods, an exam despised by the women tutors, covering four subjects. I remember only that there was a paper in economics, which I aced by relying on the understanding and notes I had gained from the course offered at Downe, and another in Latin, which I crawled through, greatly relieved that a mediaeval Latin text was an option. Early English people, it appeared, had written rather the sort of Latin that I might have written.

At the end of that first term, just before the exams, I suffered a catastrophe. I had washed my hair, set it (more or less) with some old combs, and was lying on the floor studying and drying it in front of a portable electric radiator. The combs, alas, were made of celluloid, an early and very inflammable plastic, and suddenly acrid fumes let me know that combs and hair were smouldering. By great good fortune, Ann Faber was there, studying with me, and she did all the right things. First she took my towel and put it over my head – it continued to smoulder.

She next dragged the floor mat over me – still no effect. Finally, she grabbed a jug and ran down a long passage to the bathroom for water. It was only when she poured this over that the asphyxiating smoke stopped. Blackened handfuls of my hair came away. I clearly had a bad burn, though I don't remember much pain.

Not knowing what else to do, I went to the bursar, who called a doctor. The latter's first remark was that she had not seen a burn for years but she had been called to three that day. I have long thought it likely that the other two did not survive, judging by her ineptness in my case. My own behaviour was also unintelligent.

Ann Faber

Boarding school expectations led me to think that it was the bursar's job to take care of my needs. A lifetime of excellent health care predisposed me to trust the doctor. In any event, I was determined not to miss the exam. I sat it with a swelling head covered with a white handkerchief, although otherwise properly clad in sub fusc, the obligatory all-over black clothing, topped with gown, that was required for such occasions.

By the time I reached home ten days later I was in bad shape, with fragments of melted comb still adhering. Despite my mother's skilled but excruciating ministrations – I remember no comparable pain in my whole life – I developed septicaemia. I was only saved by the availability – in a physician's family – of an early antibiotic. Although effective, it was accompanied by violent nausea, exacerbating the pain. I was not able to go back to Oxford until halfway through the following term, and then only because I insisted. The idea of forfeiting my whole year, and falling behind my cohort, was unbearable. Back in Oxford, unwilling to trust a local doctor, I cycled weekly up to Headington to have the dressing changed by a senior surgeon colleague of my father. When it finally healed, I was left with a bald patch, over four inches long and two wide. It was one of those things that 'could have been much worse', but certainly no asset to a young women who already thought herself unattractive. For a year I wore a little skull cap or combed my hair over the bald patch. This was fortunately at the back (but somehow the wind always blew from behind). My brother Douglas, luckily for me, was working with Thomas Kilner, a leading plastic surgeon who was doing what he could for the young pilots so terribly burnt as their flaming aircraft fell from the sky. Douglas arranged for me to have surgery with him, some eighteen months later, and again I rode on the coat tails of wartime medical innovation and family medical influence.

After Pass Mods was over, our first two years were dedicated to working our way steadily through English (barely British) history from Anglo-Saxon times to 1870. In 1939 it was understood that nothing since 1870 ranked as history. There was also at some point a course in philosophy and another in a period of history over which we had some choice. Every week we wrote a paper, sometimes two, if required by another course being taken concurrently, and attended an hour-long tutorial, two of us together. In these we read our papers and met with gruelling commentary from Miss McKisack, or another specialist in whatever period we had reached. At some time there was also a special research paper. Mine was on Piers Plowman; I enjoyed it but did not impress Miss McKisack favourably.

Our grounding in early history was substantially based on deep study of *Stubbs' Charters*. We were obliged to buy this fat book of mediaeval constitutional documents and encouraged to make it twice as fat by having it interleaved with blank paper for our notes. Except for lectures on Stubbs, no attendance at lectures was required. But at the start of every term our tutor made recommendations, based mainly on the scholarly reputation of the professors, rather than on any direct relevance to our current studies. The offerings had shrunk in number and quality because of the war. Individually, we probably averaged attendance at about two lectures each week. I enjoyed and benefited from some, and a few led to interesting conversation.

All of this was more stimulating and interesting than it sounds, although I found the discipline of hours of solitary reading difficult. But what I learnt during my three years at Oxford – and not least the discipline – has been of value to me all my life. The third year had a new dimension; we embarked on our all-important special subjects. It was understood that the extensive required reading would be done mostly during our summer vacation. Fair enough, the whole school year consisted of just three eight-week terms, interspersed with two vacations of six weeks and one of nearly four months.

History at Oxford had a strongly mediaeval bias, and my inclination towards more modern topics was increased by the fact that I had missed some crucial groundwork when I was absent for the first half of that second term. Now at last I had a real if limited choice, and I picked Peel's Ministry, 1840–1846, the most 'modern' of all the available topics. I set to work to read my way through a substantial list of documents: Acts of Parliament, reports of the Poor Law Commission and of the Public Health Commission, works by Engels on the one hand and Cooke Taylor on the other, Parliamentary debates and petitions on the Corn Laws, and more, and more.

Even the wartime gloom and my over-active conscience did not do away with all the youthful pleasures of Oxford. Together we regularly went to repertory plays at the theatre, cycled hither and yon, rose early on May morning to canoe or punt down river to hear the madrigals sung from high up on Magdalen Tower, and timed our trips to lectures to coincide with the brief availability at a bakery of something known as 'lardy cakes' or at a confectioners for chocolate-covered ginger pieces. Perhaps I recall these treats particularly vividly because the food at College was so bad. I particularly remember the arrival every Tuesday of wooden boxes of fish from Grimsby, which then sat in the gateway making their presence increasingly apparent until Friday, when the contents appeared at dinner. The bursar's academic qualifications made her a better fit as a member of the Senior Common Room than it did as a dietitian.

Men were scarce, boyfriends almost non-existent. I was taken to the Oxford Union by an unappealing man from Plymouth who my father said I should be good to because his father had been disgraced in some way that I never found out. Ann's engagement continued but Alan was seldom around. My brother George visited from his training unit with friends crammed into a tiny car. I had tea at Worcester College with a previously unknown cousin, and I scored a brief triumph by being asked out by a young man who came to lectures once a week in uniform. This last came to be known as 'Jo's soldier' but he was as inept as I at relationships. We had little conversation and only one kiss – his wooing consisted of asking me unexpectedly if I believed in free love? Taken aback, I said probably not, and I never saw him again. A romance developed between Joan and Morgan, the young Somervillian and the Magdalen student, who had been on our 1939 Geneva adventure. They married but he was later killed.

The war provided its own interesting distractions, although mercifully, Oxford was never bombed. We all learnt how to man a water pump; I was part of an inept college pump team. With a friend, I made sandwiches for a nearby Royal Air Force Unit, and could not believe my luck when I was asked to drive a van out to their station. This was a new van, rather different from my mother's small staid car, and equipped with power steering and power brakes that threatened to send all the cups flying whenever I put one or other foot down. My friend and I gaily signed up to drive our van down to Portsmouth in the event of an air raid emergency, telling neither our tutor nor our parents, neither of whom would have permitted it. Fortunately for everyone – probably including the inhabitants of Portsmouth – our team was never called upon for this service. It was enough of an adventure to get to the RAF unit and back.

I looked for other volunteer work. Some was expected from all of us, but I felt driven by my unremitting awareness of the war. During my first year I spent as much as two mornings a week at a day nursery. Later I spent my Saturday afternoons going for walks with children evacuated from the poorest parts of London, a small group of six-to-ten-year-olds who had proved 'unbilletable'. This meant they had been rejected by the families to whom they had initially been sent, as incorrigibly unclean, uncivilised, prone to wandering, apt to thieve, or perhaps in some instances just incurably unhappy: in any event, damaged and unmanageable. This dozen or so of assorted little people were housed in a vacant shopfront, ill-equipped for the purpose and understaffed.

They had come to rest in a good place. The matron of the hostel – I'll call her Jane – showed her love and wisdom from my first afternoon there. Rather than taking advantage of my presence to give herself a break, she sent me out with only three or four of the little boys, explaining that it was good for them to spend time in a smaller group – and also perhaps aware that I would find it challenging to handle even so few. On that first afternoon I allowed them to talk me into a visit to Woolworths. Here I lost Robbie for twenty minutes, and finally got back to the hostel hot and bothered and feeling stupid. Jane calmly told me that it had all probably been for the best as Robbie was known to be light-fingered but seemed to have returned empty-handed, which she took as a sign of improvement.

My Saturday afternoon happenings were good fodder for conversation over dinner in College, though it was only then that my sense of humour came back; during the adventures I was often in a state of near-panic. My little boys constantly embarrassed me: They would plunge down into a subterranean men's public urinal, leaving me hovering awkwardly on the brink trying to get my courage up to ask a passing man to make sure they were coming to no harm (and doing no damage). They rang doorbells and ran away. On another occasion I had to ring someone's doorbell myself, begging for use of a facility for a genuine case of sudden diarrhoea. In public parks they went wherever a sign forbade – I learnt to turn away when a park official approached, pretending I had no connection. Occasionally my friend Katherine Bruce came with me. She would never take a separate group – I was foolish enough to think she should – but it was much more enjoyable when she was with me.

After our outings, the children had their tea, sitting at bare wooden tables in the shopfront. On one occasion, waiting to be served, someone began to bang on his enamelled metal plate with his spoon, and gradually all joined in, banging in unison. I thought the noise dreadful, until Jane showed her delight in it – it was a breakthrough to have the children taking part in any cooperative activity. I was learning. I had already realised that the unpredictable activities of the walks were generally not high-spirited mischief but random acts of rudderless boys.

The girls I found to be of another ilk. I had little to do with the very few of them who were there. I found them devious and unlikeable – and then I learnt that already sex was the only coinage they knew. The world was for these children a meaningless wilderness full of people who could not be trusted. Jane had created a relatively safe space out of chaos, supplied a measure of the structure they needed, and informed it with undemanding love.

I was more interested in politics than most of my friends. The Junior Common Room committee put up a notice in the hallway asking for names to represent the College at a coming meeting of the National Union of Students. Democratic process was served by a casual process of writing in a name on this posted list and supporting it with check marks: one person, one tick (the honour system carried to extremes). A dedicated handful of Communists usually took care of NUS representation, and already had their candidate's name up, supported by a handful of ticks. When I mentioned to my friends that I might be interested, they duly added my name and their check marks (keeping to an honest count, I hope). By the time the much more deserving Communists discovered that there was a rival, the JCR had removed the list and I was found to have a majority.

Miss McKisack, who had reluctant oversight of the funds allocated for my conference expenses, was alarmed. She, like most of my fellow history students, was passionately interested in mediaeval politics but did not want to touch contemporary student affairs. I reassured her that I was not a communist, and in due course, off I went to the large NUS Conference in Birmingham. My memory of the formal sessions is that the hotly contested division was between Communism and Christianity. In my own mind – and I had given some thought to this – they were not opposites. I saw theoretical communism as having similar aims for the good of mankind as ideological Christianity, and recognised Soviet Communism as being as distant from the ideal as organised Christianity had come to be from the gospel. It was a useful experience, but I contributed nothing.

If I was somewhat at sea in the formal sessions, I was much more so in navigating the city of Birmingham. I arrived after dark, and unfortunately at much the same time as General de Gaulle, for whose safety the blackout had been made more profound and security intensified. I managed to get completely lost on two successive nights, spending one, in desperation, in an air raid shelter. Hungry, I went into a café, but was hustled to the back as it was clear that I was too innocent for the front room. Here I had my first taste of Spam, on which I breakfasted while the owner shaved at the sink. And Spam, by the way, tasted wonderful to me – it was much more meaty than the sandwich filling we had grown used to. When, the next night, I at last reached the right area for my billet, my search was made tense by a wandering soldier who followed me. It was a relief to reach the house, although it was a surprise to find that I was to share not just a room but a bed with another student. Education takes many forms.

Meanwhile, the bombing of Plymouth continued. The first few vacations back at Mount View were noisy and distracted. There were air raids almost every night. The sirens jerked us out of sleep, the drone of the bombers grew louder and the deafening noise of the anti-aircraft guns began. We made our way to the air raid shelter, which proved to be a little more distant from the house than was ideal. As we walked down the path through the trees we could sometimes hear potentially lethal shrapnel from the anti-aircraft guns pattering down through the leaves. In the morning we would find these sharp, shiny bits of once molten metal.

Another dimension was added when firebombs came into use. One way or another, we all had some training in the use of a stirrup-pump. Although water was still needed to deal with the fires that the bombs started, when phosphorous bombs replaced the first incendiaries, sand had to be used in place of water. Harold fire-watched every night. The rest of us took it in turns to watch with him. Instructions were not to put out fires burning harmlessly, in the hope that this would mislead the bombers into thinking that they were off target, hitting only open ground. So we watched a small fire here, a small fire there in our beloved garden, and only went into action when one started in the house – which happened about five times.

Once, Nannie, doing a last round of unoccupied rooms after the raid was over, smelt burning when she opened the door of the spare bedroom, and saw a round brown patch in the ceiling above the bed. Amazingly, that bomb had burnt itself out just before it would have come through. Nannie was particularly affronted – and also relieved – because resting on that bed was the whole set of new slip covers that she had just completed for the drawing room furniture. They had taken a long time to finish because of wartime priorities. I was not at home the night that Plymouth burned, but my family watched as fire spread across the whole downtown city, followed by heavy bombing, leaving nothing of the streets I had known as a child.

A serious fire was started in our roof on one of the nights I was watching with my father. I remember the challenge it was to my courage to continue to carry pails of water (this must have predated the phosphorus bombs) up the steep back stairs for him, and down again to fetch more, amid the deafening cacophony of anti-aircraft fire and the periodic screech of another stick of bombs. Outside there were fires all round. I encountered a distraught young man whose urgent need was for a pail – his house was on fire, he had access to water, but he lacked a way to carry it. I gave him the one I was carrying – a 'slop pail' of the kind used in the strange prewar days to carry the urine from the chamber pots always found under the beds of us gentry. I fetched another bucket and forced myself to go on carrying water up those stairs. It seemed noisier and more scary at every step. The noise was almost the worst part, although most of that came from 'the good guys', our anti-aircraft guns. But every now and then we heard a stick of high explosive bombs coming down – a series of screeches, thuds and explosions, sometimes each one louder than the last, which could be bad news. Harold thought he was losing his battle with this particular fire and called out that it was going through to the room below. Fortunately, it stuck on one of the thick old walls and with the liberal application of water, it burnt out, slowly but relatively harmlessly.

After one heavy raid, I didn't feel like going upstairs to bed, and lay instead on the drawing-room couch (but carefully not right under the chandelier). The electric clock on the grand piano was still going, but when I opened a sleepy eye, it was inexplicably earlier than when I had dozed off, and earlier still next time I opened my eyes. So much was out of kilter in my world that I could almost accept this – though I finally worked out that an instant's interruption in the electricity had set the clock off in the wrong direction.

During air raids, while we – my father and whoever else was keeping him company that night – were waiting for something to happen, we rested on deck chairs in the curious little lobby just inside the front door, the chapel-like one with the cherubs high up on the walls. During a lull, Harold, now chronically sleep-deprived, would doze off in his chair. He had exceptional hearing – mine was only good – and would hear the first scream of a bomb coming down before I did, and order me to get down on the floor where we remained until that stick had finished its pattern – screech, thud, scream, thud, screech, thud. During one near miss an explosion shook one of those solid little cherubs off the wall, striking Harold on his head, leaving a substantial dent in the tin hat he was fortunately wearing, as we all did. I was not there that night.

When at last the 'All Clear' sounded, we returned to bed, except for Harold, who would set off for the hospital, often on foot – because of the broken glass and sundry obstructions bound to be encountered on the roads – to perform emergency surgery on the night's casualties. Returning to breakfast one morning, he sheepishly told how, as he had reached the end of the private road on his way out, he had heard the swoosh of a bomb and then of another, and had lain down, got up, lain down again, and finally realised that the swoosh he was hearing was the repeating rush of water as the small municipal reservoir across the street struggled to keep pace with the demand of the fire-fighting population.

Not so lucky – but of course more fortunate than many – was the young minister of a new nearby Presbyterian church who was fire watching in the open near his church on the moonlit night a new weapon was deployed. Seeing a parachute coming down, he ran towards it, anticipating giving aid to a distressed airman, friend or foe. But what the parachute carried was what we came to know as a 'land mine' (not to be confused with the kind buried by armies all over the western world) – a large bomb set to explode on contact with the ground. This one took out much of his church, and stripped him of almost all his clothes. He told the story with humour, and with thankfulness for his life.

The same night, one of these new bombs landed in our kitchen garden, located at the far end of the property, sending our produce flying. Because it was at the highest point of our land, the blast passed more or less harmlessly over our house. But it blew all the windows out of the house across the road, which was occupied by the Roman Catholic bishop of Plymouth. My mother, driving out next morning, felt an irrational sense of responsibility for the damage done by 'our' land mine. Seeing the bishop outside surveying the mess, and picking something up, she stopped and called out apologetically to him. He looked up cheerfully and called back that yes, he had lost his windows but he loved onions and he had never seen them in such plenty since the war began. My mother did not dispute the ownership of the flying onions he was so pleased with.

By the beginning of my first long vacation, Mount View had suffered enough damage for my parents to have to move out – temporarily, they hoped. My father and Nannie went to stay with cousins a little farther out of town. My mother chose instead to stay with a new friend with whom she worked in the St John Ambulance. For Harold this was a hardly bearable separation, by no means alleviated by frequent lunches together. Jo's choice had been in part a snobbish one: her friend was 'county' and a cut above my father's cousins, in her view. But she was also understandably engrossed in the work she was doing.

The long Oxbridge vacations had their origin in the need for students to return home to help with harvest and other chores. By the twentieth century they had become largely leisure time for many, although serious students (and that included all women students) used the time to get through their required reading. The war caused a shift in attitude, and I rejoiced in the chance to experience a spell of 'real work' wherever opportunity arose. Just before the end of my first year, Miss Willis wrote to ask if a couple of us, history students, would go back to school and take up the work of a young teacher who had fallen ill (rather alarmingly, with a 'nervous breakdown'), for the final six weeks of the school term. Ann Faber and I took on the task. For me it was an opportunity to experience classroom teaching under Miss Willis's rather over-ambitious eye. I could not always live up to her expectations. But it was a pleasant interlude.

We were too well-fed. Downe had a new cook who not only made good use of the local produce but used up all the extra supplies that had been laid away. One weekend brought a young Frenchman, still in his teens, who had managed to escape Paris, which he had made too hot for himself by constant harassing of the Nazi occupiers. He had arrived in England knowing no one and had finally found his way to Downe, where his aunt had been the ferocious Mlle. Agobert of our prewar days. I hope he remembered the weekend he spent with us with as much pleasure as we did. It was somehow a young and joyous weekend.

We had a few rotating duties outside of our classes. I happily did more than my share of these because Alan, Ann's fiancé, was stationed not far away. Some of the other staff criticised Ann's absences, but no one was the worse off for them, and I can only be thankful that I helped to allow them some time together.

The war was always close. I was called to the phone one morning, and immediately I was sure that one of my parents had been killed. I even recall thinking that I would know which one by which voice greeted me. My mother said carefully, 'There's been another raid', and went on to tell me bad news, but not as bad – to me – as I had feared. The grounds at Mount View had indeed received a whole stick of bombs; the gardener, fire watching outside, had been killed. Mr. Collins had moved in with his common-law wife and two teenage boys not long before this, when his own downtown home had been bombed. The cottage had now been destroyed, and the house badly damaged by the near miss. My parents must get what they could out of the house. I came away from the phone in tears of relief that my parents were still both alive, and ran into a colleague who scolded me for weeping – as she thought – over material damage.

I left at once and spent a week at Mount View helping pack up whatever I could. Mr. Collins' body had been blown up into a tree by the force of the blast. The two boys had been in the cottage. I have a vivid image in my mind of the cottage ruins, with none of the jagged walls standing more than four or five feet high: how the boys survived unhurt I don't know. There was more to the family than we had known. Seven young girls had been living there with them, some of them refugees from other families in their neighbourhood who had also lost their homes in the downtown bombing. All of them had come through this raid, perhaps in the shelter, perhaps in one of the house cellars.

The raid had been almost limited to our grounds, and the police put a night watch on for one week. An off-duty policeman and his wife whose daughter had been much helped by my father (she had been born with a cleft palate) worked with us by day amid the dust and debris of fallen ceilings. My mother had found a farm that could let us have one large room of storage space. I was assigned the task of sorting books. Many went straight to paper salvage, and I know my historical understanding was insufficient to do even an adequate job of selection. But it mattered little as it turned out. Once our one farmhouse room was filled up, our goods went into a barn. Rats, it transpired, love glue, and most of the books that were not shredded were reduced by the end of the war to a pile of nibbled loose pages.

The damage at Mount View was too extensive for repair. Property owners were not allowed to spend more than a small amount on such work. To Harold's relief, he and Jo were reunited (together with faithful Nannie-of-all-work) in a small rental house nearby, and here I went when term ended at Downe. I came from Downe with a small honorarium, the first money I ever remember having earned. I spent it on a pair of blue hushpuppy shoes, then a new and highly desirable fashion – practical too because they were comfortable as well as stylish.

Shortly afterwards, Mount View was saved from falling into ruin by Keyham College, the Royal Naval Engineering College at Manadon, not far away, which took it over and restored it for use as an officers' mess. What they did for it went beyond merely rendering it rainproof. They covered all the ground floor floors with heavy linoleum and they went to some lengths to make the décor look good – on one brief visit, I saw a sailor with a watercolour paint box carefully painting a damaged spot to match the surrounding wallpaper.

During the next vacation, I served as a letter carrier over Christmas, working with a young woman newly appointed to a previously all-male preserve. She was very proud and conscientious in her job, where she was following a family tradition previously limited to males. She cared for the Post Office, she knew and cared for the people on her round, even holding back a menacingly official-looking letter for one day rather than risk delivering bad news on Christmas Day (yes, we delivered on the holiday). She teased me for my accent, but not unkindly. I would have given anything to have been able to drop my well-educated speaking to be comfortable with the local accent.

My brother George who had been conscripted into the army, reluctantly took a commission, and had been shipped off to India. But while he was on his way, the whole world was further darkened by the entry of Japan, and the USA, into the war, not long before that Christmas. George was redirected to Burma, arriving in time for the retreat. The role of the Royal Engineers was to bring up the rear and blow up bridges behind the retreating troops. He found himself suddenly with a lot of responsibility, making decisions, protecting the troops, unable to do anything for the desperate civilians who also crowded the roads. At home we had no news for many months. British and family tradition prevented us from speaking much about our fear and sense of loss. I only slowly realised how much my mother was suffering. We siblings had always known how much she cared for George, more than for either of us – that did not matter now, but we could not comfort her, nor could I share my own deep anxiety for my very dear brother. After some months we learned that he had walked out over the mountains with a handful of others, each carrying the small sack of rice that was all that stood between them and starvation. Mercifully he had avoided capture, which for so many led to death on the Burma Road or in a prison camp. Finally behind the Allied lines, he collapsed with severe malaria. His first letters were barely legible or intelligible – but he was alive.

For a while, Lorraine, the wife of my older brother Douglas, and their baby, Richard, lived with my parents. Lorraine was very young, only one year older than I, and had made a courageous choice in staying in Britain to continue her studies as a nurse when her parents returned to India at the outbreak of the war. But she had not gone on to complete her qualification, marrying my brother instead. They had been fortunate in having a couple of years together before he was called up, but now he was expecting soon to be sent overseas. He asked me for advice (a very rare occurrence); did I think he could leave Lorraine in the care of our parents? I firmly said no. I knew something of how tense and insecure Lorraine was and I knew a great deal of my mother's certainty that she was always right – particularly, as it turned out, in regard to child care. So much for asking my advice. My brother remained conservatively convinced that 'a man should be able to leave his family in the care of his parents'. Lorraine became so strung up and protective of her baby son that, whatever the time of day, he would start to cry whenever the siren sounded, and was more rather than less restless when she picked him up. To give them all credit, when she moved out, too many months later, it was accomplished without serious bad feeling.

The war affected accommodation at Oxford, also. Customarily, students spent all three years in residence, but the Radcliffe Hospital next door had taken over one building for the duration, and so the College found bed-and-breakfast billets for us in nearby streets. This meant for our second year I and three or four other Somervillians had rooms in a house on Clarendon Street. I liked my room, which had ample cupboard space. We shared the only bathroom – and toilet –and a sort of sink fitted over the bath was where we had to wash our dishes if we had tea or even – heaven forfend – had guests for a makeshift meal. The house had a rather unprepossessing landlady called Miss Sermon, who presided over breakfast daily and over our bathing privileges. We were entitled to take baths in college (not more than three a week and keep the hot water below the painted red line), and could also arrange with Miss Sermon to take a bath in our digs. I did this once, a major performance. Katherine (in full, the Hon. Katherine Bruce) also went through the process, which involved Miss Sermon's clearing space, subjecting the bath to a rare cleaning, and getting up early to set the gas geyser going. The rest of us decided it was all too much trouble, but a few weeks later Katherine asked at breakfast for a repeat. After a moment's shocked silence, Miss Sermon said, 'But, Miss Bruce, you *had* your bath!'. Katherine managed to insist without damage to her dignity or Miss Sermon's. The rest of us dared not look up from our breakfast plates.

By the time the next long vacation came round, academic pressure was mounting. McKisack would have preferred us to dedicate the whole vacation to study, but I think few of us did, though my vacation began with a few useful weeks still in Oxford. A fellow student, Joan, and I earned our accommodation by spending a couple of hours every day helping the assistant bursar – even then we had to pay a few shillings daily for university dues. Our chores were not heavy. Somerville, always desperate for funds, had, for the first time, contracted to offer accommodation to the Holiday Fellowship, an organisation that provided reasonably priced holidays for people's annual break. So many of the usual locations were out of reach because of wartime restrictions that they had decided to come to us instead. Early each morning Joan and I made up the lunches that they took with them. The Baby Bursar (as the assistant was known) provided us with the materials: wartime bread, scant margarine, an unappetising imitation of sliced meat, perhaps an apple. We set to work to make up the packages of sandwiches. Before we had time to finish, she was apt to rush back into the room, complaining that we were too slow, and divide the lunches into packets to go with groups for different destinations. We learnt to work very fast, trying always to do the crucial counting and dividing operation ourselves before she reappeared. One of her first efforts had resulted in a dozen elderly folks who were to spend the day in a bus, barely getting out for some gentle sightseeing, receiving the thirty lunches intended for a hearty all-day hiking party who came back very hungry and cross.

More interesting work came my way later that summer. I had gradually given up any hope of being clear on a call to pacifism. It might well be the better path, but I could not set my foot on it at that time. I never attended the Quaker Meeting in Oxford and gave up Meeting in my Plymouth holidays as well. The final challenge came with a call for volunteers for what would be yet another new experience for me, a paid vacation job as well – and what felt like a final renunciation of any call to pacifism. A team at the Radcliffe Hospital called for students to work in an arms factory. It was placed, like most new ordnance factories, in an area (in this case, on the edge of Liverpool) where the thirties had seen serious unemployment. The factory was experiencing much illness among the workers, and the government could not be sure whether this was due to chronic ill-health or continuing bad living conditions or was a toxic effect of the high explosives.

We were to be guinea pigs, healthy bodies, thoroughly tested before and at intervals throughout, to see what effect the work might have on us. The task was filling anti-tank mines with high explosive (TNT, tri-nitro-toluene) in a mixture of solid and liquid forms. I never sorted out my ambivalent moral feelings. I was never unaware that what I was doing was killing people, and to this day, I still occasionally wonder whether an old mine, buried in the desert sands, may not be causing someone's injury or death. I suppose I had options, but I could not, or did not, make sense of any of it. I think I may have decided at this point that I was not, and never would be, as good a person as those I most admired, and set to work to be as good as that second-rate person could be. An odd and inadequately thought-out philosophy, but I lived with it. It was many years before I again felt worthy to set foot in a Quaker Meeting, where I fairly soon found that Quakers are the same mixture of good and bad as other folks, and that like me, many had had to experience war first hand before they could find their way to pacifism.

Meanwhile, here was another opportunity for a new experience, radically different from what life would normally have brought me, and I entered into it almost wholeheartedly. After extensive testing in Oxford, about a dozen of us, the first batch of volunteers, went off to Liverpool. The factory health team were pleased to see us. They showed disrespect for and some fear of the uneducated common workers. They maintained that the workers, around whom we had better tread with care, were too ignorant and hostile to be used as experimental subjects. They nearly frustrated the purpose of the main research by urging us to try a barrier cream for our hands. They also subjected us to a few more tests, with less delicacy than the Oxford lab had displayed. I recall being handed a small test tube (in a mixed group) and told to go off to the loo and urinate into it.

We were accommodated in a new, empty hostel, spread out over considerable space, and so new and functional in its appearance, with elevated utility pipes running between buildings, that it looked to me like something out of the future. I do not know what was its planned use – probably accommodation for hoped-for American troops. The factory itself was another revelation, a mixture between a mediaeval hand workshop and a modern nightmare. Each low single-storey building held three or four workshops and a melting room. Between these buildings were substantial manmade hillocks, designed to limit the damage of any accidental explosion. Within the workshops all the filling of the landmines (which closely resembled angel-food cake pans) was done by hand, with the aid of wooden and aluminium tools, irritatingly but necessarily blunt to avoid the risk of sparks. Entering the factory area, we shed our normal clothes and put on overalls with no metal fasteners, we covered our hair with a denim scarf, and we stepped over a barrier into special shoes on the 'clean' side. From here we walked to the workshop along the 'cleanway', a smooth surface without a speck of grit on it.

The workers in the shop were almost all women, though a few men worked in the back where some of the TNT was melted down and put into steam-warmed cans for us to use to fill in the spaces between the broken chunks of solid material – looking for all the world like a light fudge that Nannie had made with me in the nursery – so that the cans would be packed solid. The space in the middle was for the detonator, not part of our responsibility.

Our fellow workers were not hostile at all. They treated us with unfailing courtesy and friendship. They appreciated that we were there to help in some way, although they found it hard to believe that we had actually come so far of our own choice. They showed us the ropes in every way, and during our one major mid-shift break took us along to the cafeteria, where we all sat, eating our dinners and listening to piped music. Smokers could even catch a cigarette during the break, lit from a fixed electric lighter. The hit song of the time, in which we all joined, was 'The stars at NIGHT (clap, clap) are big and BRIGHT (clap, clap) deep in the HEAAART of Texas.' The US troops and their music must have been on their way. Any real or imagined love interest among the students was greeted with delight; 'No snogging on the cleanways!' they warned us.

All the workers had had hard lives. They had lived through the Depression and were still living in poorer parts of Liverpool, in many cases raising young families, glad of a steady wage and putting up with a good deal to earn it. We worked on a three-shift rotation, changing shifts every week. I cannot imagine why this was the routine. And the night shift was the longest, and it felt it. Though friendly and accepting to us, the workers saw the administration as another culture, almost as the enemy. What physical danger there was arose in part from this. Danger inspectors circulated through the factory, looking for spent matches accidentally brought in, or hairgrips that might cause a spark if trodden on. We always had good warning of their coming – they were to be outwitted. The manual of regulations was no help because it had been written between the wars for ordnance factories under no pressure to speed up production. Mines, according to the manual, were to be placed at least six inches apart, and were to be handled with great care. I admit I was startled the first time I saw an experienced worker pick one up and bang it on the floor to dislodge TNT that had congealed in the wrong part of the tin can. The tables were closely covered with full cans, the walls lined with piles of completed mines. The fact is that TNT does not explode easily. Accidents in this type of factory were rare (though comparatively minor ones too frequently maimed workers where the detonators were made). The regulations had been eased in the interest of maximum production – the inspectors were no longer bothered by lack of space between mines – but we hardly knew which ones were still important. I still have my doubts about the wisdom of banging cans full of high explosive on the floor. Any explosion would have caused a major catastrophe with significant loss of life.

The centre of public news during our few weeks at the factory was the battle of Stalingrad. Russia's heroic stand against the eastern advance of German troops had a visceral as well as a political appeal for the workers. Here were fellow workers, liberated by communism, standing up to save the world. Churchill, no lover of the Soviets and not yet able to open the longed-for second front in western Europe, must have had a sour taste in his mouth as he shamelessly exploited the opportunity. No longer was the Communist Party undesirable; the Internationale was sung, the Red Flag was flown throughout the country. As for us, we competed between workshops to make the most mines in every shift, to save our comrades in Stalingrad.

Shortly before the end of our time in the factory, one of the students went down with mumps and was removed to hospital. The day we were due to leave I realised that I was also developing the illness, the only one of the common contagious children's diseases (measles, chicken pox, whatever) that I had not got out of the way during my boarding school education. I could not bear the thought of spending time in hospital in a city where I knew no one. I was able to travel back to Oxford by train, with the help of a co-conspirator, Peter T. He was noted for his ardent pursuit of Maria C, a Maltese student, more made-up than the rest of us, but undoubtedly head and shoulders more gorgeous than any of us could ever hope to be. Peter had known her for some time, and was eager to become engaged, but Maria was not ready for this. The resulting cooling-off freed him to take care of me on the trip back to Oxford. He also devised some strategy to discourage other passengers from sharing our compartment, short of telling them that I was a risk to their health.

The Radcliffe laboratory welcomed us eagerly. I was feverish and feeling very ill by the time we arrived. The junior researcher who met us said I had probably better just be counted out of the experiment and sent home. The lead researcher instead treated my illness as a piece of good fortune, declaring that one theory was that the ill effects of exposure to TNT would only show up in people who were otherwise unwell. So I stayed overnight and went through the whole battery of tests next morning. Then I cabled my parents, 'Arriving at 4:20 pm complete with mild mumps'. I crept on to another train to sit huddled guiltily in the corner until we reached Plymouth, where I was given an undeserved welcome and tender care, despite the inconvenience of my arrival with a contagious disease. Lorraine and baby Richard were still with my parents, and elaborate arrangements had to be made to separate me from them until I was out of quarantine.

Recovering rapidly, I enjoyed showing off my yellow hands and my copper curl. Most of us had followed the fashion among the workers and left a small amount of hair outside the obligatory scarf, nothing as extreme as the 'canary girls' I had seen in Liverpool, those who worked with the volatile picric acid used to fill detonators, putting up with bright yellow skin on hands and faces, and daily facing the risk of maiming explosions.

Later, I learned that the Radcliffe experiment had yielded useful results. Part way through, the technicians had found that the volunteers who worked in the melting room had a rapid rise in white cell count. Daily blood counts (some of us volunteered for these extra pricks) confirmed this, leading to the conclusion that damage was done primarily by breathing the vapour, and not, as they had speculated, through the skin. Exposure could easily be diminished (not eliminated) by issuing masks to the workers in the melting room, and by preventing the other workers from lining up inside the steam room (sometimes for considerable periods) to fill their cans.

The rest of the vacation was given over to study. I took a subscription to the amazing London Library, a private library that had (and still has) a massive collection including all the nineteenth-century volumes of Hansard and Acts of Parliament that I needed. At that time the library's main function, other than as a library and club for members living in London, was its mail service. You could borrow a substantial number of books at a time which came promptly by mail, you could keep them for a considerable period (perhaps until someone else needed them?) and then mail them back (I became an expert parcel-packer). None of this was, to my knowledge, adversely affected by the war. I could not have worked my way through all that material without the London Library.

Back at Oxford, we settled down to the grind of preparing for our final exams in the coming June. In all our three years we had had no official exams or papers that would count towards our results, and only one practice run of tests, put on by the women tutors for the women students. Limited places for women ensured pressure to keep the standards up on those of us who had been fortunate enough to get into college. The final exams would cover the content of the past three years. Here again, I think my choice of a modern specialisation was a disadvantage. Although Miss McKisack put us through a rigorous review of the earliest history, I could not get into it the way the mediaevalists could.

At age twenty-one in June 1943, I was a more mature student than I had been at eighteen in October 1940. Back in college, I now had a room I loved, high above the front courtyard, with a dormer window and a useful large glory-hole cupboard – I have always needed some such place to help me keep my innate untidiness under control or out of sight. I took out my neglected watercolours one evening and painted – on foolscap essay paper – a picture of the window, with its shabby blackout curtains, my simple desk, and the wooden bowl I still had from the Buckland Common bowl man. I still have this picture (and the bowl). It may be the best picture I ever painted, catching the soft light and something of my reflective mood.

One evening, I had an unexpected visit from the college porter, bringing me an urgent message. He was taken aback to see Ann Faber, who was studying with me, but he did the best he could. He gave me only a London phone number, not the name of the caller. I hurried down to

*View from my Somerville window, painted on foolscap
essay paper*

make the call on the public telephone in the hallway. It was Lady Faber: Alan, Ann's fiancé, had been listed as missing in action at the battle of El Alamein. She asked me to break the news as gently as I could to Ann. Ann had of course recognised the number, and when I got back I found her shrunken and huddled in the chair. She continued to hope against hope, as does everyone who gets this foreboding but not quite conclusive news. It was weeks, if not months before Alan's death was confirmed. Ann's heart had not been in her work all year, and now she lost all interest, although she struggled on.

I, meanwhile, found myself in the unusual position – unusual for me, and rare even among my contemporaries in those man-less days – of having a more or less regular boyfriend. Or an on-and-off boyfriend. Peter T had attached himself to me, and I was on the whole enjoying it, although he made it clear that his heart was still with Maria. I suppose in some ways it suited me. I certainly did not want a committed relationship, particularly as Peter was a devoted Roman Catholic. He was a physicist, exempted from the armed forces in part because of the importance of his work, and in part because of progressive deafness, about which nothing could be done at that time. He was good company. We went for walks together, indulged in a good deal of 'petting' but nothing further (his Catholic awareness of gradations of sin was helpful here). We talked endlessly of all manner of things, including, as I remember, trainspotting, jazz and religion, even of the Catholic insistence (at that time) that spouses become Catholic and that children be raised in the Church. We did not talk of his work, which was secret. It embarrasses me to recall how freely I tolerated his constant comparison of myself to Maria (I was pretty, she was beautiful), but at least I knew where we stood. Every now and then she found time for him for a week or two. Before long he would be back to spend time with me. Meanwhile, I had a date for a May Ball. Peter took me to University College, where we danced till late to live music. Afterwards, I climbed into College over the wall, one of the very rare times that I did this, because the rumoured penalty was being sent down. Late permits could be obtained (once a term) until midnight, but this too would have spoilt the evening. Climbing in was fairly easy. The wall was high but the railing on top had been removed and sent for war scrap metal.

During one vacation I spent a couple of weeks with my Aunt Lizzie, who was living a lonely life in a tiny hamlet called Drumelzier near Peebles. She had been keeping house for her younger brother George until he joined the army as a chaplain. As Matron of a hospital in Hertfordshire, she had enjoyed a position of considerable power and dignity, but on retirement her pension was meagre, and had now diminished with inflation. She went wherever she could be of use in return for a bare living. Soon, my father would quietly commit to

In the courtyard at Somerville, showing wartime vegetable production. And Jo

providing a permanent small addition to her income. Within a day or two of my arrival, I heard from Peter T announcing that he was coming to join me, would stay in a nearby village and come to Drumelzier by bus daily. I broke the news to my aunt and her only visitor, the local ghillie, who came by frequently to make sure that she was all right. Peter and I walked in the glen daily. I was well on my way to falling in love with him. In the evenings the ghillie embarrassed me by making remarks to my aunt, redolent with dour Scottish humour, about what he might have seen in the glen that day.

During another vacation Peter visited me at home. I will always associate him with walks in the wild places. We spent wonderful days on Dartmoor, making use of what transport was available: country buses, a very rare lift from my father, or best of all, the small narrow-track railway that ran from Dousland to Princetown, the bleak little town in the centre of the moor, that held Dartmoor Prison. On one occasion we even flagged this train down from the hillside as it approached a seldom-used

A peaceful interlude in wartime. Photo by Peter T

request stop. We drank rough cider in pubs, we dreamt impossible dreams about a lovely stone house on the bank of the Tavy near Walkhampton, inexplicably abandoned to fall into ruin. Beside it there was an old round cider press, made of a solid granite wheel that had been pulled around the granite trough by a pony, the whole under a lichen-covered slate roof.

My father must have been worried. He was a dyed-in-the-wool Protestant and would have hated me to marry a Catholic. But he handled it well, expressing his liking of Peter and leaving us to work out our problems ourselves.

In June came the final exams. As ever, it was the hottest week of the year; we had to wear sub fusc, all black (or by a wartime concession, navy blue). I think I sat nine three-hour papers in six days. Not blessed with a particularly good memory for exam recall, I had worked out ways of study, making use of suggestions that had originally come from Jean Rowntree. I identified topics, not specific questions, and organised the facts and an outline of dates for each into a small compass no more than would fit on a postcard. I memorised this outline, and had it available in my memory. Now I had the factual data ready to apply to whatever question came up, and could focus on making sure that I used them strictly to address the form of the question. Ideas were more important and came more readily once the facts were not at issue. Besides the essay questions, there were, for my special subject, what were known as snippets papers (two, I think), consisting of a lot of short quotations from all those documents I had pored over, every one to be identified, with a comment on its significance in some issue – a very thorough test of knowledge of facts and comprehension of ideas, as well as of familiarity with the documents.

Before the war, the Oxford exam in history had been followed by a 'viva', an oral exam. My relief that this had now been limited only to those who were on the cusp between two grades was short-lived. After I had been home for a few weeks, I was called back to be vivaed. Only two of us history students from Somerville were summoned, Rosemary Mitchell and myself. Rosemary was a brilliant student, one of several May McKisack had hoped would do her credit with a first. We met back at college. Rosemary was a nervous student who had thrown up daily during the finals, and did so again on the morning of the viva. I too was seriously scared at the prospect of the viva, but I nonetheless went over the wall again – to meet with Peter – on the night before, feeling that nothing would make much difference.

The viva was not too bad. Although it focused almost entirely on the early mediaeval period – as I had feared it might – I thought I acquitted myself well enough. Grading at that time was done in a way that still seems to me less than objective. I could see my exam marks on a paper before the examiners and I saw very high alphas against my special subject papers. But I guessed, rightly, that Rosemary, who received quite a grilling, was swinging between a second and a first, and I between a second and a third. No grace was given for her nervous condition and when the final results came out a week later, we both had seconds. McKisack, disappointed in the results of what she had seen as a very able year, let us see the courtesy note she received. I was relieved that I had made it to the second class, though I found it (and still find it) unnecessarily patronising that the note said that the viva had been to give me a chance to *raise* myself to a second. I had no grade below a beta – –, and my special papers were alpha + and alpha ++. As for Rosemary, I heard later that the examiners, determined not to allow the war to degrade standards, had given only one first-class in history throughout the whole university that year, and that to a Rhodes scholar who already had at least an undergraduate degree from a reputable United States university. Two of our Somerville history year had gained only thirds: Ann Faber, whose heart had not been in it, and Katherine Bruce, very bright, but disappointed in the content of her special subject and too bored to force herself to read all those documents. So I know I was at the bottom of the seconds, eighth in the Somerville class of ten – but a second is a second and I was not forced to tell anyone. Years later, when I went back to academic study, teaching and writing, I realised that Oxford had taught me how to study, and notably how to do research from original documents.

Now it was done, and I was to become part of the war effort at last.

CHAPTER 11

After University

When I graduated with my BA from Oxford there was no ceremony – as far as I remember. In due course, a smallish, simple certificate arrived in a cardboard tube, marking the end of the academic interlude. I wonder if I even showed it to my parents. It seemed something of so little significance in wartime.

We were spared the angst of having to find a job, much less of anything as weighty as having to determine on a career. We were directed – conscripted – into whatever field was deemed to lack labourers. The Women's Army Corps and the Women's Royal Naval Service were not in need at the time, and in the view of the government, any post-secondary education fitted us for one or other branch of the Civil Service. Several of my friends working in sundry offices in Whitehall were designated as 'Principals', misleading indeed, but a notch higher and slightly better paid than my position. I was an Assistant Inspector for the Ministry of Health in a local office in the heart of the City of London. Never mind, I think I had the better experience.

A team of about seven of us under an Inspector were charged with administering the creaking machinery of the old prewar Health and Unemployment Insurance Acts passed in 1908 and 1911, all their obscure amendments, and innumerable mystifying modifications introduced since. We were much more than arm's length from anything directly related to health and illness. The job of us juniors (of whom I was the most junior) was to make sure that employers in our area stuck stamps on the health and unemployment cards of all qualified employees. More satisfying – though equally ritualistic – work was done from time to time by the more experienced members of the team. They were charged with trying to track the record of some elderly person who was now desperately in need of an old age pension and might – or might not – have accumulated the right to one by her long but intermittent work as a 'char' for a dozen different employers. The employers, if we could find them and they were still in business, were often full of good will and enjoying wartime prosperity and so were more ready to add a half dozen stamps than they were willing – or able in prevailing circumstances – to recall whether it was for six or eight weeks that Mrs. Jones had scrubbed the floor of the shop or the bar. Sometimes it was hard even to confirm that it was Mrs. Jones at all, since what records they had showed the

149

name of that temporary worker as Mrs. Johns and she was now calling
herself Mrs. Jones. The genuine permanent civil servant, Marion, whose
office I shared and who was my appointed mentor, took me along on one
or two of these investigations and explained all this to me. She stressed
the importance of sticking scrupulously to the rules and getting at the
facts, however much you wanted to help. She was right, of course, and
herself a lovely caring person whom I remember with affection and
respect.

For routine inspections, my daily work, each of us had responsibility
for all the businesses within a group of streets. A great bonus for me was
that my area was an old part of the City, including the ancient steep
mediaeval lanes (such as Pudding Lane and Fish Lane). These led down
to Billingsgate, the fish market, on the shore of the Thames, where you
had to take care not to step out in front of a hurrying fish porter with a
stack of five baskets on his head, full of the morning's catch, doubly
precious in wartime. And where you had to find out and record the busy
opening hours of the pubs, which had a special dispensation to serve
those thirsty fishermen at the hours convenient to them.

The value of horse-drawn drays as a major form of transportation of
goods was unquestioned in wartime. I would see steaming, sweat-flecked
carthorses straining to pull a heavy load up a steep incline, their hooves
striking sparks from the cobbles. A number were stabled beneath our
office building, and occasionally, chancing to return by that route at
dusk, I was scared and thrilled by a team of the huge animals thundering
in behind me at a canter, if not a gallop, as they anticipated their evening
feed.

Once in a while I sat on a stool in the fish market and discussed
insurance stamps with someone while he de-winkled winkles from their
shells. The exercise was very good for me, shy as I was and unaccustomed
to approaching strangers. I found it much less of a challenge than walking
in cold to a small business and insisting on seeing all their current pay
documents. The conventions surrounding compensation for work turned
out to be deeply entrenched in the class system. So, indeed, were health
and unemployment insurance, which did not have to be paid – or, to put
it another way, were not available – for those above a certain rate of pay.
Fair enough, employers readily showed you their wage books, in which
were written the amounts paid weekly to Bill and Marnie who worked at
the 'working-class' jobs such as storage, carrying messages, rubbish
disposal, cleaning. Salary books, however, were another matter and were
shown reluctantly. What distinguished salaries from wages was not so

much the amount paid as the supposed superior nature of the job and the frequency – or infrequency – of payment. Wages were paid weekly, salaries came monthly, sometimes even quarterly – as, if I remember rightly, was mine. And salaries were private. I never experienced the unpleasantness of outright refusal that some inspectors warned me about, but it was not uncommon to have to insist.

For me the novelty of the situation was good, and working conditions very pleasant, several hours every day out and about, one or two spent writing up undemanding reports, chatting with Marion. Also some time spent perhaps reading through the latest print-out regarding the proofs needed to establish the insurance eligibility of out-workers in the box trade – that is, of women who made a few shillings folding boxes in their own homes, a trade which had virtually disappeared in wartime. The atmosphere in the office was relaxed. We came in at 9 am, went about our business, and nearly all departed by 4 pm, some of us carrying our briefcases and murmuring something about 'making another call on the way home'. It was not what I had expected in moving out into the world of wartime urgency. Now that I had found myself to be ineligible for the calling of a pacifist – which I still saw as a high one – I was fully committed to the war, and had hoped that graduation would see me engaged in some meaningful way in the war effort.

Meanwhile, I worked as best I could at this, my first real job. My little patch of the city was all on record in a small file box, with a card for every employer. I was supposed to visit each one, and to take two to three years to cover the whole, being careful not to turn up on anyone's doorstep too frequently: 'Employers don't like it if you're there too often', I was told.

My patch had been neglected for a while, so there seemed to be plenty to do. But as I began to work through the cards I came up against the consequences of the war. The worst of the London Blitz was over, but our area, so close to the Thames, had been hard hit. Many small import businesses had ceased to exist, and others had moved away or merged. Even more significantly, not only many single buildings but whole small streets had been turned to rubble. More than one third of the streets in which I was supposed to be visiting employers no longer had a single business in them – some had no buildings – others had two or three in place of the dozen or so for which I had cards. Marion told me that she believed our work anyway was unnecessary in wartime, pointing out that Scotland, bound by the same Health and Unemployment Insurance Act, had abandoned inspection 'for the duration'. The remaining employers were enjoying some wartime prosperity and were unlikely to save a few shillings at the expense of their hard-to-get employees. As a permanent civil servant – a respected, coveted and hard-won job before the war – Marion now felt trapped. She longed to leave but was unable to. She knew she would not get the Chief Inspector's support if she tried.

Meanwhile, I went on working. Without pressing myself, I was soon polishing off the inspections on the remaining businesses fast enough to see that I might soon work myself out of a job. This was fine with me, but not with our boss. Her rank depended on having at least six of us working under her, and she would have been hard put to find something else for me to do. I worked the same hours as others in the office and recorded them on my monthly time sheet. After two or three months, I was called in to the Chief Inspector's office for an evaluation. The Inspector, a kindly woman but acutely aware of the tenuousness of her position, spoke well of my productivity and of the neatness and lucidity of what reports I had written and then added, in carefully chosen words, that there was one thing which needed to be improved. 'You are', she said, 'not putting in enough hours'.

From then on, finding myself unable or unwilling to record hours that I had not worked, I really did 'put in more hours', spending still more time working through my streets and staying an extra hour every day in an empty office. But now I knew I had to leave.

I thought about embarking on training as a nurse, which I found would be acceptable to the Inspector because of some curious logic linking it to our mandate of 'health'. Not surprisingly, my request for further training was turned down. I knew well that I was more drawn to medicine than to nursing, but I lacked the needed scientific preliminaries and reluctantly turned my back on any kind of medical career – for good, as it turned out.

My mother was talking to her naval friends, and let me know that recruits were indeed again being sought for some categories in the Women's Royal Naval Service (WRNS). Between us, we managed to arrange for my call-up. Once my official redirection was confirmed, I let the Inspector know and was duly scolded. But she could not keep me.

Looking back on all this, I have nothing to be proud of. I am glad I found myself unable to comply with the expectation that I would sign for hours I had not worked, but I had done nothing for the public good. I blew no whistle, rang no bells, confronted nobody. Before I left, I finished off the routine inspections of all my allocated area. And now, just five months after I started work and a few days before I left, another young woman graduate arrived to take my place. I wonder what she did for the remaining two years of the war.

Outside working hours, this had been rather a lonely time for me. I had found myself a pleasant room in a house in Hampstead, with use of the kitchen, which I shared with my landlady. Several members of the WRNS, from Canada (I think) also lived there, but they had their own self-contained apartment and anyway found me completely uninteresting. We barely spoke. I had planned to take the opportunity to try some recipes and teach myself to cook, but soon found it boring when I never had a visitor, so I didn't cook beyond just adequately getting myself something to eat. Generally my only company in the evenings was the landlady's parrot, who resided on a perch in the kitchen, and whose conversation was limited. My landlady was pleasant but understandably more interested in the Wrens than in me. They were well-dressed, more so than I would be when I later became a British Wren. My landlady did not improve my self-image when she offered me some of their castoff Canadian brassieres, pointing out what they might do for my figure.

I looked for companionship. I went to the local church on Sundays, wistfully thinking of the pleasure my father took in inviting any stray serviceman home for lunch after Sunday service. Fortunately, I did not have to stay in London every weekend. More successfully, I reached out to several of my cousins, farmers in Essex and within easy reach, and spent enjoyable weekends getting to know family members I had scarcely met before. Since my father was the youngest among his many siblings (and had not married young), my cousins were all older than I and were now raising their young children. Most were evangelical Christians, and I found myself reproved by a seven-year-old for offering to sew a button on for her before Sunday chapel. Once I was called on to lead a Sunday school class, where I met with another aspect of the class system. My cousins were 'gentleman farmers'; the religious lesson was for the children of the working peasants, not for their own children. The routine was to hear them recite the Bible verse assigned the previous week and assign another, no more, no less. My attempts to explore or enhance their understanding of the meaning of the verses learnt by rote were out of place. But I enjoyed these weekends. It was good to get out into the countryside, even if we were still in sight of the Dagenham motor works. Sometimes I even got to ride on horseback through the fields with my cousin, and would catch a glimpse of a less settled, more restless side of my staid cousin.

I learnt, too, to make use of what wartime London had to offer in the theatre – an impressive choice, as it turned out. Shaftesbury Avenue, Drury Lane, Leicester Square, the Old Vic itself, names to conjure with, with theatres here and there standing up to the threats and inconveniences of wartime with remarkable resilience. Among the actors I saw were a number well on their way to the top: Laurence Olivier, Ralph Richardson, Maggie Smith, John Gielgud in a variety of plays – *Oedipus Rex*, Shakespeare classics and new plays by such as T. S. Eliot. Sometimes I went alone, sometimes I was able to meet up with Ann Faber, also temporarily a civil servant (though later she too managed to convert into a Wren, a torpedo technician). Some theatres set aside limited seating in the gods for very inexpensive purchase on the day of the show. I got up early – really early, maybe 4 or 5 am – and made my way to the West End, where I stood at the front of any line there was. When the hatch opened, at 6 am, I was greeted by a caretaker-cum-ticket seller. The first question of the caretaker I best remember was always 'What time did you get here?' I think she took a sadistic pleasure in pushing the hour back and back – she was always ready to tell you of even earlier arrivals and suggest that you were lucky that you were near enough to the front to buy a ticket. And, at that, it wasn't really a ticket, just a coupon for a small folding stool that she would set up in line to hold your place until the real box office opened in the evening. I never heard of that sacrosanct little row of empty stools being violated. Rushing there after work, you could be assured of your place at the front of the line. If the art of queuing was perfected in wartime Britain, this must surely have been its apex.

I spent the occasional weekend with Peter and his mother at her home in Pinner, not far from where I was living. She tolerated me with difficulty, and always set me to work at darning his socks, which were so worn that I was darning on darns. Peter told me he had in fact spare pairs put away but she was determined to preserve these for some ultimate emergency. Peter was the younger of two sons. I never knew who his father had been or what income sustained his mother or had paid for his good education at Merchant Taylors' School. Of his mother's origin, all he would say was that she came from 'central Europe'. Although she seemed to me to be whiny and demanding, I see now that she may have done well by her boys in what must have been a difficult life.

Peter was still glad of my company, and I of his. Maria was more or less out of the picture – but not out of his mind – and, with his characteristic urgent need for female friendship, Peter was seeing a good deal of another woman in Oxford, named Blue. As ever, he openly discussed his relationship. We never tried to exact any commitment from each other, and our physical relationship meanwhile remained constrained by the religious moralities in which we had both been raised and in which we believed, mine Protestant, his Catholic. And also, to be frank, we were both constrained by fear of consequences, he of eternal damnation, me (in those pre-pill days) much more practically, of pregnancy.

The end of that story was the mirror image of the stereotype. I went off to join the navy, and a few months later, Peter let me know that he had married Blue. As far as I know – and very much hope – it was the right thing for him. Marriage between us certainly would not have been. Retelling the story has put me in touch with a valuable component Peter brought to our relationship. He was honest with me. Not faithful, not always considerate, just honest.

CHAPTER 12

The Fleet Air Arm

As soon as I was free from my brief stint with the Ministry of Health, I was called up by the Women's Royal Naval Service, to report for basic training on the shores of Loch Lomond, where I spent a cold February (1944). There were two basic training camps, the other at Mill Hill in North London; later, comparing our experiences with those of Wrens who had gone to Mill Hill, I was sure that our conditions had been much harsher.

The camp consisted of a number of Nissen huts in the grounds of Tullichewan castle. The castle was a classic gothic revival monstrosity, built in 1792, and demolished in 1952. Our officers lived in the castle itself, where I am sure they were at least marginally more comfortable than we were. We slept on bunks in the Nissen huts, about twenty to a hut; washing facilities were in similar huts. The mandatory blackout was achieved by a device that automatically shut off the light every time the door was opened, contributing to the chaos of our early rise in the morning. Our days were divided between squad drill, which I perversely enjoyed, lectures and physical work. The only time I saw the inside of the castle was when I had to scrub the floor under the eye of a Petty Officer, when I desperately wished my education had included more of a practical domestic nature. I did not find floor-scrubbing beneath my dignity (as a few of my companions did), I just wished I could do it better and didn't feel such a fool. Few of the lectures were interesting. One officer would impress the importance of punctuality on us ('navy time is five minutes before time'), the next would arrive 25 minutes late. We did gain some understanding of navy structure and routine, and of what our life would be like. It was interesting and useful to learn, for instance, that we would receive a free packet of sanitary towels every month, courtesy not of the navy, but of an anonymous private donor. I still admire the genuine generosity of whoever it was that was willing to give such an unnameable gift, and equally the courage of whatever senior Wren officer had drawn her attention to the need.

The categories being recruited at that time were cooks and stewards, and air mechanics. I was excited to find that I was to become an air mechanic. Most of those going in as cooks and stewards came from the poorer areas of Glasgow, so were not far from home – though farther than they had ever been before. One exception was a girl who arrived a day late, coming from the Outer Hebrides – and speaking only Gaelic. She was, I think, a year or two older than the other cooks and stewards, most of whom were very young; volunteers could enter at sixteen years of age, compulsion began at seventeen. Most, but not all, of the potential air mechanics were girls who had attended private schools and were at least a couple of years older (though not as old as I). The thinking was that our education would help us better understand the mechanics' training, and may have worked satisfactorily in that respect, although the logic is not clear, since male mechanics were largely drawn from ordinary state schools. Perhaps I was a snob among snobs, as I remember thinking that I didn't particularly like the sound of the

*By the end of the war, nearly everybody was in uniform
My mother was in the St. John Ambulance Unit*

private schools my fellow recruits had attended. But I did have some justification for finding some of them picky and superior in their attitudes, and meanwhile I was learning. I spent the few spare evenings we had with the youngsters from Glasgow. In the intervals of running screaming from boys who threw snowballs (I was naïve enough at first to think we would do better to ignore them, not realising that the chase was the purpose, despite the screaming and protesting), my new teenaged Glasgow friends asked me what I did in the evenings at home? Where did I go? Did my mum let me go to the movies with my boyfriend? My stumbling replies earned their pity: 'You haven't been around much, have you?' they said. In a sense, they were right. Most of them had been working or looking for work for two years, since leaving school at age fourteen.

The climate at meals was something I have not experienced before or since. There was never quite enough food (what there was was good) to satisfy the ravenous appetites we built up with hard exercise in the cold air, and sharing was not every one's priority, so you learnt to sit down near at least one substantial source of nourishment – the bread plate, the

Douglas was in the Royal Army Medical Corps

main course platter, the pan of soup or porridge, or at worst the common jug of treacle. Highlights were when some extra fried bread appeared; hunger makes appetite and I have seldom tasted anything as delicious.

Uniforms were not issued until after two weeks, so squad drill saw a raggedy unmatched bunch of girls marching to shouted orders up and down the icy parade ground. It also shed an unexpected light on recent social history. The squad was organised in height order. I had always been one of the shortest in my school class; now I found myself exactly placed between the private school girls and the Glasgow girls. The Depression had taken its toll in inadequate nourishment. But not of the spirits of these young women; they took everything as it came, and reacted spontaneously. For the first week most of them were homesick and vowed they would not stay after the month was up – the teenage volunteers did have this option – but by the second week they were eager to try on the new uniforms and learn to tie a tie – made rather painful for all of us by the substantial reaction to an ill-timed compulsory inoculation. Tullichewan was a training station for cooks and stewards, so many of the Glasgow recruits would still be close to home for a few weeks longer.

At the end of our month at Tullichewan, those of us who were to be air mechanics were packed off to *HMS Fledgling*, in Staffordshire. We now had not only our basic navy blue skirts and jackets, white shirts, black ties and thick black stockings – our dress uniform – but serge bell-bottom trousers, dark blue shirts (for winter), white square cut short-sleeved shirts for summer, and a fine duffel bag in which to carry it all. The bell-bottoms and the summer shirts were the standard issue supplied to male sailors, with no concessions made to differences in the female anatomy. I can't see the design of these trousers as having been particularly convenient even for men; the front had large flaps folding over from each side with a third flap pulled up and buttoned over them – no fly. We were also provided with a small sewing kit, so we all set to work to do the best we could to modify these garments. I was quite skinny in those days and had no pronounced female figure, so it wasn't too hard just to slit the white shirts up at the side and to cut away some of the bulky three layers of serge at the front of the trousers. I grew fond of my bell-bottoms. For some women they were hard to adjust and must have remained inconvenient and uncomfortable.

The training was four months long, well designed, thorough and well taught, mostly by petty officers with practical experience of servicing the aircraft that flew from aircraft carriers. There were four categories of air mechanic:

George was in the Royal Engineers

ordnance, electrical, airframe and engine. Before I left school, Miss Willis had tried at one point to redirect me into science; this had resulted in several sessions with the senior science teacher, who had felt put upon, but had tried to find out what I was interested in. The one question I had been able to come up with was that I would like to understand the workings of the internal combustion engine. For some reason this was not science to her so it had led nowhere; so I was more than happy now to become an engine mechanic. It was, in fact, deeply satisfying to me to be confronted with a clear explanation and simple diagrams that solved the mystery of how the energy of fuel was converted to the thrust of engine. I already had more experience with simple tools than most girls, and the practical side of the course was equally a joy.

Conditions in *HMS Fledgling* were much better than at Tullichewan, except for the food. We took turns, on a roster, at dishwashing and at scrubbing the floors of the kitchen and the enormous dining room. The food was plentiful – as it should have been, since navy rations were substantially more than civilian ones – but so atrociously prepared as to be barely edible. There was no sign of the mealtime competition we had experienced in Scotland. The wastage was exacerbated by no account being taken of likely levels of consumption: meal after meal, a big pan of some unpalatable mess was served to each table, however few people had sat down at it. Meal after meal, three quarters of each dish of burnt rice, half cooked potatoes, tough meat, curdled custard, was scraped into the overflowing pig bins, that practical wartime expedient to raise extra food. The local pigs must have been the fattest in the nation (supposing that pigs can tolerate ruined food). Meanwhile, many of the trainees skipped meals and wrote home complaining to their mums, who responded with parcels of home baked goods, squeezed from their own scant rations. There was no adequate supervision of the cooks and stewards; a minor irritation was that we ate only margarine while the domestic workers enjoyed our butter rations as much as they enjoyed bossing us around when it was our turn of kitchen duty.

And I was in the Women's Royal Naval Service (Fleet Air Arm)

Eventually, several trainees in the class ahead of mine, and gifted with more political know-how than I, found a manual on procedure and put it to good use next time a completely ruined meal was served, making a formal complaint to the relevant officer, interrupting her own peaceful meal in the officers' mess, cooked by its own kitchen staff. She was obliged by protocol to come and taste what had been served, and when she found that indeed no part of it was fit to eat, the cooks had to prepare another whole mid-day dinner. The whole class schedule was thrown off for the day, and everyone was inconvenienced, not least the floor scrubbers, of whom I happened to be one. But the kitchen staff and, I presume, the responsible officer, took their responsibilities rather more seriously; some slight improvement resulted. We had all had a chance to learn something about how not to be helpless.

My class of Engine Mechanics under training

160

Somehow I had my bicycle with me; I suppose I had simply asked my parents to send it by rail, and in those pre-technological days, there were some systems that worked better than they do now. In my free time, I cycled down to the nearby village, Hovingham, within walking distance, but so much more easily accessible to those of us who had wheels, and found my way to a pleasant canteen run by the local people, where for a few pence you could get tea and a snack, and more blissfully still a few quiet minutes in a different environment.

For me the canteen led to a new friendship; after a few embarrassing moments on my first visit, when I realised, after enjoying my snack, that I had left my money belt in my cabin, I was 'adopted' by the local doctor's wife, Elizabeth Starling, who made a practice of providing a home from home for a member of each successive *Fledgling* course; what a gift.

Elizabeth Starling had held an aircraft pilot's licence before marriage, and was envious of the opportunities we now had, though she did not seriously question her traditional role as a doctor's wife, and as the mother of two small girls, all of which she performed admirably. I liked her husband, Evelyn, but he was of course always busy. I provided some relief from unremitting childish conversation and Elizabeth did not ask anything more from me – I don't think I as much as did any babysitting for them. I remember the celebrations of children's birthday parties, and even of one

Evelyn and Elizabeth Starling, Helga and Josephine, who befriended me when I served in HMS Fledgling *in Staffordshire*

specially given for me. Elizabeth's wartime cooking was accident-prone. On one special occasion the cat got in and ate most of the precious sardines off the crackers (we salvaged what we could). On another, a cake, lovingly prepared with a rare egg, dried fruit, and other hoarded ingredients looked beautiful but proved impossible to cut; Elizabeth had mistaken a packet of powdered gelatine for demerara sugar. Feeding a family and providing treats was so hard in wartime that Elizabeth found it hard to keep her sense of humour in the face of such disasters. For me, the Starlings provided a time out from the war, a brief visit to life as I had thought it would be. We kept in touch off and on for a while after I left: I learnt of the birth of a boy, and then with sorrow, of the sudden death of Evelyn from a coronary. I regret not having kept in contact for longer than I did; I never saw Elizabeth again after I left *Fledgling*, and we lost touch at the end of the war.

At *Fledgling* discipline was still strict. I remember two students who had some trouble fitting in. One was a girl who was – or considered herself to be – from an upper-class family. She was more accustomed to ordering other people about than to following orders promptly and unquestioningly as we were expected to do. She did odd things like trying to travel first class on a train trip, and she simply did not understand that the ordinary rules and obligations applied to her. Perhaps she had never as much as attended a regular private school, much less been to boarding school. Possibly she deserved more pity than she got from any of us, but she won no friends by her attitude of superiority. After two or three weeks of constant confrontation with authority, of confinement to barracks, of other routine punishments, and of being the constant subject of gossip, I do not remember hearing more of her. I wonder, did she settle in? Or did the navy give up on her and ship her back home?

The other Wren who excited a good deal of interest was a very different case. Celia was a sixteen-year-old, fresh from boarding school, whose sister was one of the *Fledgling*'s officers, and whose parents had allowed her to join on an understanding that her sister would be able to keep an eye on her, at least during the training period. This was a completely inappropriate and unworkable arrangement, unfair to everyone concerned, especially to the youngster, who was likeable, well-behaved on the whole, but found herself bound by a set of rules within rules and the proneness of her sister to pop up behind her shoulder at any moment in the role of anxious and admonitory mother hen.

One of the few forms of entertainment available was dancing, something we all loved to do. But there was a limited supply of men. The very best dance was held at the parallel institution to *Fledgling*, not far distant, where we met with young men taking a similar training to ours. But dances there were rare – I only remember one; we had a good time (though I recall that Celia's sister had enlisted the help of an officer of that unit to make sure surreptitiously that she did not drink or get led astray).

Jo Vellacott

The shortage of men was filled by the American troops now pouring into Britain, and spending a few weeks in Britain acclimatising as we all awaited the opening of the western front. Many were in temporary barracks or hostels of the kind I had been in in Liverpool. We provided a convenient pool of available dancing partners; invitations were frequent and welcome, although there was an unflattering and curiously commercial ring to them: a notice would go up asking for Wrens to attend a dance at such and such US army unit, with spaces below numbered one to thirty, and a note that trucks would be outside at 7 pm. The dancing was fun, especially if there was a live band; frequently partners stayed together the whole evening, and you had a chance to chat. A few real friendships developed from these structured occasions, but the odds were against them. I remember one evening spent with a slightly older-than-average man (perhaps my own age? I was twenty-two that summer) and finding we had a lot in common; but he was not on the make, and when I told him, in answer to a question, that I had a boyfriend, he would take it no further and did not suggest another meeting. My relationship with Peter T was too complicated to explain (we were clear that we had no commitment to one another) and perhaps I did not need to be so honest.

My partner's restraint was rare; it often became evident that the evening was not only about dancing: many GIs had roving hands and moved fast. Going outside for a breath of fresh air often provided some relief. On one evening this was reversed. We had been invited to a pub by a group of GIs who had evidently been grumbling because they were not dancers and so had no way of meeting girls. They soon demonstrated that 'meeting' was an understatement for what they wanted: on this occasion they were in a hurry to find a partner and get her outside in the dusk. They were mostly mildly drunk, tedious and aggressive – but not violent – and in the main we managed to get them back inside or to take our walks with another couple, providing a measure of protection. We hailed the return of the truck with some relief and boarded it gladly. But the roll call revealed that the unfortunate Celia was not with us. No one knew where she had gone and quite a hunt ensued, while we sat in the truck, many, I regret to say, heartlessly chanting 'Celia's missing, Celia's missing'. Eventually she returned; she had been sitting peacefully on a hillside, enjoying a chat with a young man who was not much older than she and, I fully believe (though few did), just as innocent. I am sure it was all duly reported to her sister.

At the end of our course, we each received an appropriate symbol to sew on our jackets, and, a great delight to me, our own wooden toolbox, equipped with a serviceable minimum set of tools; spanners, hammers, screwdrivers, pliers. And off we went on our first home leave.

I do not remember much of that leave, except the pride with which I showed off my toolbox. Our graduation must have been close to D-Day, when the Allied forces began the massive western front invasion of Europe. I was impressed, and a little envious, to learn that Felicity, now a cypher officer, had been among the invading forces. A recent school presentation by her granddaughter, Ellie, confirms that she was among the first twelve Wren officers to cross (and that a suitcase with all her clothes was accidentally dropped in the Channel on the way). Few of my close acquaintance had remained in the civil service jobs to which we had initially been sent; Ann was now a torpedo Wren at a station in Scotland.

My journey south had been without incident, but the trip at the end of my leave, to my new posting in Crail, Scotland, was quite an adventure. My mother took me to the railway station and embarrassed me by pulling strings with her railway friends – known to her through her good work as a liaison officer – to get a corner seat for me in an empty compartment on a very crowded train. However, at the last minute, after we had said our goodbyes, the compartment was taken over authoritatively by a naval picket party, consisting of a Petty Officer and two ratings on a mission to retrieve a man who was Absent Without Leave and was being held for them in Glasgow. With some condescension, they decided to let me stay, as I was 'one of them'. Such a picket party was only designated for a particular occasion, and was not part of any ongoing naval police force. It soon became clear that, while they were committed to the job they had been set to do, this particular party were also determined to make the outing a bit of a spree.

Our rail route was soon in trouble. We were diverted because overnight bombing had taken out part of the main rail line, so we travelled very slowly by a different route, eventually reaching Birmingham, where I knew I had to change trains, late in the day. We were all turned out of the train at that point and waited on the platform for some hours – with a three-deep crowd of anxious travellers – before the next northbound train drew in. My escort took one look at the packed train and decided they did not have to fight their way on. At my insistence they obligingly manhandled me and my baggage into the last space in the corridor, where I crouched uncomfortably on my tool box, clutching my duffel bag, with no room to move in any direction. The train slowly drew out – and then drew back in again. One of my new friends appeared at the door and told me firmly, and with some kind of wink, that I did not have to travel on that train, and pulled me and my baggage off. They had found that farther down the train a whole section had been reserved for prisoners of war under guard, who conveniently did not appear, so we took over not a mere empty compartment but a whole carriage, space enough for all to take a longed-for nap. To give credence to their claim, one of them had taken on the role of man under arrest, removing his canvas gaiters (the mark of picket duty) and ready to have the handcuffs put on if authority was in the offing. I was placed in a corner, covered with one of their coats and topped with one of their hats, so that I could be passed off as a sleeping member of their party. We had several hours of more or less undisturbed dozing, though I didn't sleep well as I was afraid of missing my stop. I have no idea now where that was, and I was the only one awake when we reached it, but reach it we did, and I crept out of my corner and off the train with my tool box and duffel bag without waking my faithful escort, who were continuing on to Glasgow – sorry not to say goodbye and thank them, but feeling that leaving their sleep undisturbed was a better way of showing my gratitude.

On the final leg of my journey I found myself in a truck with several other Wrens headed, like myself, for *HMS Jackdaw*, the Fleet Air Arm station at Crail. By this time I had a raging migraine, and thought I might disgrace myself by throwing up during the bumpy truck ride to the base.

A special occasion in HMS Jackdaw *at Crail. Barracudas fly past*

165

I survived, though looking ill enough to be taken straight to the sick bay on arrival – where I rapidly recovered, aided by aspirin and a short, deep sleep. The rail trip had taken over twenty-four hours.

Celia's parents were not the only ones who seem to have viewed the navy as a somewhat benevolent institution, prepared to go out of their way to take care of their tender daughters. I wrote home with an account of my journey: my father sought out the unit to which my helpful pickets belonged, to express his praise and gratitude to them. I never told him how horrified I was (justifiably, I fear). I can only hope that his report did not get them all into deep trouble for the unorthodoxies of their dealings with me, let alone of using deception to ensure themselves a reasonably comfortable journey.

HMS Jackdaw was a training station perched on the cliffs above the North Sea. Conditions were sufficiently rough that it was designated as a 'hard-living' posting. The main thing I remember about this is that it entitled the men – but not the women – to a daily rum ration. Perhaps it was also why we could only 'go ashore' that is, leave the base, at designated times, when an imaginary boat was leaving.

We slept in dormitory blocks, thirty-six to a 'cabin', six or eight cabins to a unit, joined by a corridor ('gangway'), the whole served by a mess hall. Most of the time, hard work in the open air made sleep easy and mitigated any defects in the food, which was in any case better than I had seen during training. We were issued with our own 'mess traps', knife, fork, spoon and china cup (yes, china: this was before the days of universal plastic). We had to bring these to meals. Dinner plates were provided, but the Royal Navy had apparently run out of side plates, so our portions of margarine and treacle were served on saucers. When I met my mother on a visit at a hotel in Edinburgh, I had to relearn the practice of using a saucer as a receptacle for a cup; I kept finding my cup sitting awkwardly on the tablecloth.

We were woken in the morning by the bosun's whistle and an injunction to lash up and stow: there may have been more words to this, but I remember only a version I heard just once, when the sailor on duty sang to all of us, 'Beautiful dreamer, lash up and stow, how you can lie there I really don't know!' It made our day, but brought him several hours of pack drill. We slept on double bunks and shared between us drawer space in small chests between the bunks. Everything had to be left tidy. This only once became an issue, when a notice went up telling us to make sure that everything was neat on the following Tuesday. This odd wording was a warning of the coming visit of a notoriously picky senior

Wren officer, noted for peering under every Wren's pillow to make sure that nothing was there except our pyjamas. She duly came, and followed up her inspection of the sleeping quarters with a special gathering after work at which she administered a scolding on our untidy hair and general appearance in our bell-bottoms. In her eyes the WRNS had deteriorated deplorably since its early days. The captain of the *Jackdaw* chose to exercise his right to attend any event on the base and walked in on this entirely female event partway through, to her obvious (and, on his part, I am sure intended) discomfiture, speaking briefly, when she was done, of how highly he valued the work of the Wrens.

Every morning we marched down to the hangars. I was assigned to the storage section. We worked in small teams, usually one Wren with one or two male mechanics, doing routine daily inspections and the more thorough thirty-hour inspections required after that amount of time actually in the air. The aircraft were Barracudas, torpedo dive bombers equipped (as were the well-known Spitfires) with Rolls Royce Merlin 8-cylinder in-line engines (later replaced by the similar heavier Griffin engines), and with an odd-looking high tail fin. Our inspections concluded with starting up the engine, using the explosive capsule starter: this was always a thrill to me, though I longed to do much more, indeed, to learn to fly. We had learnt about both in-line and rotary engines, but at Crail we had few left of the old Swordfish aircraft, and I never worked on one. Occasionally some newer type of aircraft would appear for a day or two, exciting great interest. All Fleet Air Arm planes were built to fly from aircraft carriers; the airframe mechanics dealt with the subtleties of folding wings, and devices to catch and slow down the planes on landing.

The storage section was a good place to work, with a close comradeship among mechanics

These were the planes we worked on (postcard)

who all took our work seriously, and a good Petty Officer who knew his workers – unlike our commissioned officer, who was seldom seen and knew no one by name. The summer and autumn of that year were sunny and windy. Most afternoons, we ended our day looking after aircraft on a storage field, above the built up area, on a cliff surrounded on three sides by the North Sea. I acquired such a tan that my mother did not recognise me as I walked down the street to meet her on that rare visit to Edinburgh. During the day, we worked in an unheated hangar, a very cold place once winter came. Mid-morning saw a welcome break, when the NAAFI wagon came by with coffee and 'Naafi wads', plain white rolls, deliciously fresh on Mondays, not quite so fresh on Tuesdays, stale on Wednesdays, like a rock by the end of the week. For coffee we lined up with what we could find in the way of mugs; we had each had a mug at some point, but china mugs do not last long in a tool box, so we shared the one or two remaining, trying to get to the front of the line, quickly take a swig or two each and get in line again for a refill. It took planning. There was no running water in the hangar, so the mugs (like our oily hands) were seldom if ever washed. I am happy to say that the view of germs I had brought from my antiseptic childhood left me easily, and has never completely returned.

We had a curious ritual exchange (not limited to our small group of friends, but much used by us). As we stood around outside the hangar, cold hands on a coffee mug, or puffing on the cheap Woodbine cigarettes we favoured, someone would be sure to ask, 'Why is a mouse when it spins?', to which the reply was, 'The higher the fewer'. Or the question could be, 'How's your ma for sugar?' to which the reply was 'Up to her knees in condensed milk, thank you'. Why this meaningless exchange, always deadpan, was comforting I do not know. We were cold, sometimes wet, and dirty: but we trusted each other, and we were content.

Often we had a dance on Saturday nights. My enjoyment of these was limited because I had no regular partner, and at times was unaccountably stiff in any man's embrace, not to mention the bother of dealing with the few – never from my own storage section – who were over-eager and would attempt something near rape if you could not avoid their attempts to 'see you safely home' at the end of the dance. On Sundays there was sometimes a church parade, a chilly business as the Wrens were lined up well ahead of time on a parade ground so icy that if you were forbidden to move your feet for more than a few minutes, you would find them frozen to the ground when the order to march was given. We Wrens had all been kitted out with overcoats and raincoats, but the men had one or the other, so in order to achieve uniformity, no coats were permitted. The men were (marginally) reasonably clad in their bell-bottoms and serge overtops. We were deprived of our cosy bell-bottoms in favour of our dress uniforms of coats and skirts, leaving our stocking-clad legs exposed to the bitter winds. But I remember one Sunday on which all this was worthwhile, when we marched down to the assembly hall behind the bagpipes of the Black Watch.

On other weekends we often had a free day to go to St. Andrews, a short train ride away. Often I went with friends, including another 'Jo' and Gordon Gande, both fellow mechanics. In peacetime St. Andrews is a thriving tourist town, noted for golf course, university and historic interest. Of these I remember the ruined castle, with its grisly bottle-shaped dungeon into which prisoners had been thrown (through the neck

A day off in St. Andrews

of the bottle) to starve to death, an occasional glimpse of a red university gown (so sensibly unique in that they were manufactured for the northern climate, of warm red cloth), and an empty windswept golf course. But we knew the best places to eat; an honest wartime meal would be baked beans on toast, or perhaps a welsh rarebit, either of which contained a protein allowance within the regulated amount for a main dish. Rarely, we had a whole weekend off, and went to Dundee, we women staying in a delightful hostel where we could lie in on Sunday morning, take a comfortable bath, and enjoy a good breakfast.

Our good times of hard work and trusted companionship came to an end when a decision was made to move the storage section to another base, where there was no accommodation for Wrens. The rumour of the move hung over us for weeks, during which time the men drank more – constantly mourning the move – and occasionally risked severe punishment by smuggling out their rum ration so we could join with them in yet another dismal farewell party.

We missed our friends badly, and the authorities really did not seem to know what to do with us. I was one of several engine mechanics assigned to the airframe hangar, where aircraft went when they needed attention to the structure or a coat of paint. It was a big, comfortable hangar, adequately heated to serve the needs of the aircraft and the paint. But we had no work to do. The rare engine inspections due before a plane left the hangar were done by men who had worked there for months. Once a senior officer came to inspect the work of the section, and I was planted on a scaffold beside a plane and told to look as if I was doing something. I fantasised about a possible truthful response should the dignitary question me, but – perhaps fortunately – nothing came of it. Every day, bored Wrens spent the day unmissed in the washroom hut, where there was a small rest area beside the loos and usually a few girlie magazines to look at. I couldn't do this, more because of the intolerable boredom than from priggishness. It was no less tedious to hang about without work in the hangar, so I took to bringing a book with me and sitting quietly on my tool box at the side of the hangar, but in full view and available for work if any should miraculously materialise. For this visible inaction, I was soon put on a charge and summoned before the Wren officer responsible for our discipline (almost the only time I saw her). She reluctantly gave me a chance to explain the situation and a good result followed; most of us were transferred to other sections. We were still seldom busy, but there was usually something to do. The work was the same as in the storage hangar, but we had nothing like the work on the storage field, and no similar sense of group solidarity. I was a little fearful of repercussions from those who might resent the transfer from the comparative comfort of the airframe hangar to the unheated maintenance hangar, but I heard none, despite the increasing cold as winter closed in. The hangar doors offered little protection even when closed, and not infrequently one or other of them was blown off in a storm or by the force of an engine being carelessly started up too close by. Occasionally when work was slack, a friend, Margaret, and I took it on ourselves to clear out the tracks so that the doors would move more easily and securely. We became known as wanting to fill our time and once spent over a week, at the behest of an officer, carefully painting an oversize portable board on canvas for the playing of Uckers, a traditional Fleet Air Arm game similar to Ludo. Not, I thought, an immense contribution to the war effort, but quite fun to do; and who knows? Recreation is important to morale.

After a while, Margaret and I discovered a more exciting way to make use of slack times. We found out that we could get permission to go up on test flights. Every plane was put through a routine test flight after the longer inspections, and – no real surprise – pilots were quite happy to take along a mechanic who had worked on the plane they were flying. The Barracuda was a three-seater, with an observer in the belly of the plane behind the pilot and a rear gunner behind him, each in his separate cockpit, and all designed to have a maximum view. The test flight consisted of going up to ten thousand feet, then diving down to about one hundred feet – very hard on the eardrums – and flying close to the water, dipping wings, and testing other functions. On a clear day you could, as they say, see forever. Once I saw, far below, a small aircraft fly under a river bridge. On another, just after Christmas, I was not sure what to make of the pilot's singing 'Hark! The Herald Angels Sing.'

Margaret and I grew close, taking these flights together, getting permission, drawing a parachute, finding someone who would lend us each a helmet – though we never communicated with the pilots nor they with us, a circumstance that contributed in an odd way to the end of my friendship with Margaret and of our flights together. Going out to the plane one day we saw that the pilot was not one of the two usual rather dull test pilots; the stranger turned out to be the Commander Flying, who had taken over because he wanted to get a close look at an aircraft carrier that was standing some distance off the coast. We flew well above this for some time. How tiny it looked: but I would have jumped at a chance to experience a landing or takeoff. The pilot performed the routine tests, but with far more pizazz than we were used to, going higher, diving more steeply to barely above the waves, dipping the wings until I thought they would touch the water. Finally we were on our way home. As we came in to land, the pilot's voice came through my helmet, asking me (it was my turn in the observer's seat) to check whether the undercarriage had come down and was locked properly. I had to confess that I was not an airframe mechanic, but said it looked all right to me. However, the appropriate light on the pilot's dashboard had not come on, and presently I heard him calling the control tower. I remember his exact words, partly because even then I heard them as almost a parody of what a British pilot – perhaps in a movie – should sound like: 'This is the Commander Flying', he said in a decidedly upper-crust accent, 'I may make a bit of a prang on landing'. We flew around for a bit longer, while below, as I heard later, they scurried around preparing foam and fire trucks and an ambulance. I could see Margaret in the rear cockpit, but could not attract her attention and was not sure whether she had heard all this. I should have called the pilot, but wrongly, I now think, I held to our unwritten code of not speaking to officers unless spoken to, and of not risking getting someone else in trouble – someone would be at fault if Margaret's helmet was defective or not switched on. I felt she would be angry if I spoke out of turn. The only thing I could have done if we had confirmed that her helmet was out of order would have been to take off my parachute and wriggle along the floor of the plane to her cockpit, to warn her to buckle up well for landing, something she commonly did not do. This time-consuming exercise was something it made no sense to do without letting the pilot know. I said nothing. As we got out of the plane – after a perfectly routine landing– it was a relief to hear her say, 'Wasn't that exciting?' But my relief came too soon: she must have been referring to the departure from routine testing. We had no opportunity for further conversation that day, and the next day a mutual friend told me that Margaret did not want to speak to me. Despite a number of efforts, I never managed to have her reverse this dictate, so I do not really know what second-hand account of the incident she had heard or what it was that had so offended her. I still think I had behaved badly, but I would have liked a chance to talk it over with her, and I missed her friendship

Conditions in our living quarters took a sharp turn for the worse when *Jackdaw* was struck by a hurricane. The day before the hurricane, by chance, was declared an unexpected 'makers', that is, a 'make-do-and-mend' or free day. In the morning I received a letter from Peter T, telling me of his marriage to Blue. I decided to walk it off and walked several miles alone along the shore, scrambling over the rocks in wind and sea-spray, indulging in grief that was at least partly real. It was lucky that I turned back when I did; I reached the barracks just before the force of the storm struck. Later, reluctant to be kept in by the rising storm, several of us tried to make our way to the NAAFI café. We found that if you stood upright, you would be blown along willy-nilly with no choice of direction. The only way to make any progress against the wind was by crouching down. (And the NAAFI was closed). Several planes were blown off their moorings – one of our jobs on the storage field was to turn them into the prevailing wind and lash them down – and one of the larger ones had been blown into the sea.

We were more directly affected by the loss of the hot-water boilers in both big Wren sleeping blocks. Seemingly, they had been allowed to boil dry and had both been destroyed. I find it hard to credit that the Royal Navy could not raise a new boiler, but for the last four months of my stay on the base, and for at least another two months after I left, we had no hot water. No officers slept regularly in our quarters, and I still kick myself for a missed opportunity when I was duty Wren, a small chore that came round occasionally. A major component of this duty was to see to the needs of the Duty Officer. When that night's officer sent me to run her bath for her, I should have done just that, so that she could have had the shock of facing an ice-cold tub. Instead I explained the situation to her; she was miffed at the personal inconvenience to herself. The fact that more than a thousand Wrens were getting dirtier and dirtier was of no interest in the officer's mess, it seems. It never occurred to us to make any big issue of it. When there was a dance, some of the men brought fire buckets full of hot water to hand over the fence for their girlfriends' use; this prompted a notice warning the men not to put fire pails to unauthorised usage. The padre got permission for us to use a shower in a gym at the other end of the base, and I found time to make occasional use of this.

It was to the padre that I took a growing concern of my own. I had come to feel comfortable with him because of a small poetry-reading group that he organised, a real chance to step into another world for an hour. I was still enjoying the engine work, when there was any to do, but having to beg for work left me feeling I was doing nothing to help the war effort. When I told him I thought I might be of more use as an officer, I sensed his disapproval; he thought I was being elitist. I have to admit that I did also think I would enjoy the social life of an officer's mess, despite the fact that some of my few encounters with officers had not engendered much respect. Anyway, he recognised my qualifications as a potential air engineer officer and passed on a suggestion. It was not long before I was sent south to Worthy Down for further technical training, a first stage in the process of promotion.

Worthy Down was a fairly small air base, with one of the rare surviving grass runways and limited air traffic, but dedicated to technical training. Courses were offered in whatever was needed, for whomever was sent there to take them. There may well have been more system to it than I saw. Only two principles shaped what we did there: one sensible one was that we, the handful of WRNS air mechanics studying to become Air Engineer Officers, were directed to courses in the three fields other than our own – that is, as an engine mechanic, I must be exposed to some education in airframe, electricity and ordnance. The other was harder to comprehend or live with; it was that there was no time or measurement for when we would graduate: we would stay at Worthy Down until each of us, individually, was called to move on to formal training in the art of being a WRNS officer. I was one of the lucky ones, spending just six weeks at Worthy Down, long enough to take short courses in the various specialties, not long enough to begin to think you had been abandoned. As I recall it, the instruction in airframe and ordnance were short and specifically designed for us, or perhaps to occupy the time of an instructor who was currently at a loose end. I have a vivid memory of a good-looking ordnance instructor perched on a high stool, holding forth to about five of us, and waxing excited as he recounted episodes from his active service, spreading out his arms and in danger of swooping right off his stool as he twisted and turned to avoid enemy aircraft. I remember nothing of the airframe instruction. But the whole exercise made some sense; we picked up a smattering of knowledge, and at least some familiarity with terms relevant to each field.

The instruction in electricity was of a different kind altogether: we were thrown in with a class of twenty-five students from the Royal Navy Engineering College at Keyham (that same College whose officers were now occupying Mount View) who were at Worthy Down for a few weeks in their third year of a long university-level degree course. None of us Wrens had any background in physics, nor practical experience with electrical work; the instructor found himself struggling to impart basic concepts to us. But he recognised that what we did have was keenness and a certain amount of interest. Keyham, surely a sought after education between the wars, had become a long drawn out agony for most of the regular students, who just wished to be finished with schooling and get on with the war. They were bored, slack and inattentive. Few of them would have been destined for the Fleet Air Arm, or had any interest in aircraft rather than ships. I think the instructor knew how to make use of our unexpected appearance among them; we were encouraged to ask questions, and given good answers. We took a regular test at the end, on what had been covered in the two weeks, and acquitted ourselves not too badly. Understandably, most of the women were bunched close to the bottom of the class (but with a passing mark). But at the very top was a Wren, putting all the Keyham students to shame. This woman, called Jacqueline Collacott (a name in rhythm and rhyme remarkably like mine) was very young and brilliant and unpolished. Coming from a state school, she had already won a scholarship to Oxford, in arts, not in science, to be taken up after the war. I would love to know what became of her. I did all right, too, coming seventh in the combined class, probably more a reflection of how idle the men were than of my grasp of electrical principles and practice – but I had found it interesting and challenging and I was not intimidated.

While at Worthy Down we had comfortable accommodation some distance away in a big old house in the country, and equipped with a tennis court, which we enjoyed in early spring weather. One weekend I hitchhiked my way to the farm of a bachelor farming cousin, Warren Andrew, where I was fed the best-tasting boiled egg I had had in years by Warren's housekeeper. I went back several times, and came to know a whole new (to me) family of cousins of my father's generation. My father had, advisedly, kept us as children from exposure to this part of the family because of Warren's tendency to aggressive evangelicalism. Fortunately, he now seems to have seen me as beyond redemption and always treated me with affection and respect – although I was well prayed over in the morning prayer sessions, and teased unmercifully whenever occasion arose. A sixteen-year-old relative who was staying with him was not so fortunate, and tended to burst out with difficult questions on anything from smoking to the meaning of life whenever we found ourselves alone together.

Back at Worthy Down, it was a relief to be given orders, one by one, for our next move – a course of indefinite duration has a very odd feel to it. I was glad to set off for a month in North London as an officer cadet.

The one month officers' training had little in it that was memorable. I concede that some of it was necessary and much of it was useful, although rather too much seemed to be devoted to making sure we knew how to behave like ladies. I enjoyed a few periods of strenuous exercise, and also, perversely, of learning to give drill commands, but remember little else. Two of us were air mechanics on our way to becoming Air Engineer Officers, several were decoding Wrens, to be commissioned as Cypher Officers; the Royal Navy had sufficient Wrens who understood the codes in use, but was short of those qualified to see certain classified material, for which not mere skill but an officer's rank was deemed necessary. The course instructors were hard on them, dubious whether the fact that their skills were in demand justified their admission to an officers' mess. We spent free afternoons in the West End, being fitted at tailoring shops – I went to Austin Reed – for our new uniforms; I believe it was understood that if you failed to get your commission, the order would be cancelled without penalty, probably a rare enough occurrence to be worth the gamble for these establishments.

A couple of days before the end of the course, everything changed. The war in Europe came to an end. Excitement and relief flooded over us. And yet not completely. My brothers had survived, but Douglas was still in Europe and George still in Asia, in a war that had not ended. We cadets were allowed the free day granted by the government. I am glad to have been able to spend that very special day, with my friends, in the centre of London. Crowds were everywhere, though I fancied that I detected the same sadness as I felt under the rejoicing. So many must have been remembering lost friends and family, so many must have had ones they cared for still in ongoing theatres of war. I could not say that the war was over.

In the evening we made our way to Buckingham Palace, and waited for the King and Queen to appear. And waited. And waited, unable to tear ourselves away, but increasingly anxious, recalling the strict injunction to be back at the school by midnight; it had been made clear that any cadet who was late would not get her commission, regardless of excuses. The officers in charge of our training had not been chosen for their flexibility or sense of humour. We had also been reminded that our white hatbands made us easy to identify and had been warned that any inappropriate behaviour would not pass unnoticed or be forgiven. At last the Royals did appear, and we joined in the cheering before making a run for the Underground, with just time to make it home. But the Tube was full as I have never seen it before or since. We had to push ourselves on by sheer force, and then stand helplessly as the train bypassed several stations, fortunately drawing to a stop at the station we needed, for long enough for us to fight our way off the train. It was five to twelve and we ran as fast as we could to the school, ringing the doorbell just on the stroke of midnight. One student in our class failed to graduate; we were never told why.

After one more day came the formal graduation. Dame Vera Laughton Mathews was there to present us with our commissions. I don't recall anything of the ceremony but I clearly remember a curious ritual that took place on the previous evening. Dame Vera was an imposing presence who had served in the newly formed WRNS during the First

World War, and had been appointed to head up its second incarnation as early as April 1939. Rumour had it that any cadet who failed in the slightest way to comply with her expectations at dinner or during a compulsory recreation period after the meal would be flunked. The meal was manageable; then we adjourned to the recreation room to play ping-pong. The fixtures were the table – and Dame Vera. Each one of us in turn, alphabetically, had to play one full game against her. Fortunately, she was quite a strong player, so we thirty cadets went down as expected, one by one. Not so fortunately, I too was a strong player (all those games with George) and found myself keeping up well with her score. Tension in the room grew as we came to the crucial twenty-twenty mark. I wondered whether it was mandatory to lose? Perhaps nervousness played a part, but it was with relief that I lost – just. After that, Dame Vera worked her way through – or over – the few remaining students. We were all longing to be free to go and pack for our early departure next morning. But she was not finished with me. Because my match had been so close I was called back to the table for another game. I have never been able to lose a game deliberately, but I am sure on this occasion I did not try too hard to win, and went down to defeat more gratefully than gracefully.

At the last minute I was diverted from my expected and hoped-for posting to a Fleet Air Arm station. I was instead told that senior officers were calling for an air engineer officer from the WRNS to fill a position at the Ministry of Aircraft Production (MAP) at Millbank. The current holder, Second Officer Etty-Leal, had forcefully expressed a wish for an overseas posting, but no one had been found to take over from her. Apparently, a strong showing in the initial air mechanic's course, reinforced perhaps by some report from Worthy Down (where I had thought we were invisible) had led to the suggestion that I might fill the bill. Unusually, I was given a choice: I need not take up the offer if I did not want to. Perhaps regrettably, I was still driven by the foolish idea that what was challenging was probably worth doing. I accepted.

Socially, it was a horrible decision. Here I was, again in London, with no shared social life related to my work, and no congenial mixed officers' mess; once a year, MAP held a Christmas dinner for all its boffins and service personnel. I lived in a commandeered Nurses' Residence in Hampstead with about a dozen other WRNS officers, mostly working in Whitehall in various Admiralty departments. The residence also housed a considerable number of rank and file Wrens, but their quarters were somewhat separate and we saw very little of them, except for the few who

*A scintillating social occasion at the Ministry of Aircraft Production evening,
RDE(N) is at the left.*

waited on us in our mess. A somewhat more senior officer served as
Commanding Officer of the whole. Evening dinners for the officers were
well prepared and served with an attempt at formality. Their substance
was, I am glad to say, enjoyable but within appropriate wartime rationing
restrictions. I shared a comfortable room with a fellow officer, and she
and I occasionally went to a movie together; but much of the time I was
acutely lonely, although I again made use of whatever relatives and
friends were within reach. I had an unfortunate encounter with Peter's
mother, who insisted on having me visit her so that she could tearfully
tell me all about what a mistake Peter had made in choosing Blue. Had
he chosen me, I am sure Blue would have heard how much better a
choice she would have been.

I renewed my visits to the theatre, and had a very curious encounter
on one occasion; the man next to me, although accompanied by a
woman, spent the performance trying to feel me up, while I shrank into
my seat, unwilling to sacrifice my hard-won ticket and too embarrassed
to seek help. What was more threatening was that a week later, turning
out my over-full handbag, I came on a pencilled note begging me to meet
someone – it had to have been put there by my trying theatre neighbour
– at a certain address. The whole thing was so implausible – I was even
in uniform – that I wondered whether it was some sinister trafficking

connection and I should have gone to the police. I still wonder.

Meanwhile I had acquired another boyfriend, highly respectable but in the long run not desirable. James P was an officer at Keyham College and came to know my father as the owner of Mount View, by then in use as an officers' mess for Keyham. My father liked him, and a friendship developed, particularly when James showed appreciation of shared interests and expressed similar religious beliefs and commitment. We were introduced to each other and James followed up by taking me out several times when he was in London. In the abstract, these dates were exactly what I had been hoping for. James took me to dinner and dancing at chic places, even a nightclub. It could have been such fun and so romantic. But I could never find anything to talk about and the postwar life James looked forward to sounded to me deadly dull. I soon sensed that he was thinking seriously of me as a marriage prospect, and I found that my father and he had spoken of this (in a decidedly old-fashioned way). My father, deeply impressed with his professed faith and his general steadiness, really liked the idea. I could not see myself spending the next decades confined in James's suburban home raising James's children, even though at that time I accepted that, like many middle-class women, I might not be free to work outside the home. I had, too, a growing uneasy feeling, from the way he spoke of my family, my father, and his hopes for the future, that he thought he had found a wife with money, and expected that my father would be paying me a handsome allowance after marriage (although that was never my expectation, nor, as I found out, that of my father). I decided to disillusion him before we reached the embarrassment of a formal proposal, and I cut him off short – on a London Underground station platform – trying to be gentle and to explain my feeling that we did not have enough in common. He picked up only that he lit no spark in me and rather roughly and unpleasantly tried to demonstrate right there that he could be physically passionate. The arrival of the train was a relief. When I think back on this episode, I believe that my instinct was right, and that in fact James had started to make plans as soon as he met my father, a seemingly well off man with an unattached daughter. My father was disappointed to hear of the end of our friendship, but, as ever, accepted that I must make my own choices. A few months later James married the daughter of a senior officer at Keyham; another route to advancement?

One incident at the residence is worth recounting. I did not tell anyone about it for a long time (and never any one in my family) because it seemed to reflect credit on myself. I still think it does, but now, so much later, I can be pleased that on this occasion I acted with good sense and some courage. The handful of officers at the residence shared some responsibility for oversight of the whole WRNS quarters, taking turns to serve as Duty Officer for the evening hours, under the Commanding Officer. One summer evening, when I happened to be Duty Officer, we got a warning, just as we finished our dinner, that a man was heading for the residence, angry and aggressive, and claiming some particular reason to break in on us. A group of us, including the CO, made for the hallway. One went towards the only phone, in an alcove close to the front door, the rest of us rushed to close the double front door. Too late – the door burst open before we could fasten it or make use of the phone. We had the advantage of numbers, we had a responsibility towards the regular Wrens whose quarters were accessible through another door off the hall, and surely the CO would take charge. I tend to move slowly under pressure; I suppose I was weighing the situation. Suddenly, I found myself alone with the invader, no one else in sight. Everyone – including the one who had unsuccessfully tried to place a call – had fled back to the dining room, and closed the door. Everyone except myself.

Three things slightly reassured me: the invader had stumbled as he broke in; he was not a very big man (though substantially larger than I); he might be somewhat drunk. As he gathered himself together, we exchanged some kind of introductions. He was indeed very angry, but not with me, he was after a friend who had betrayed him and with whom he must have a reckoning. His quarry, he was sure, was somewhere in our residence and he was here to dig him out and beat him to a pulp. I introduced myself as the Duty Officer, and told him firmly that he couldn't come in, we didn't allow any men in and for the same reason I could assure him sanctimoniously that his prey would never have been admitted. What felt to me like a very long conversation ensued. I lectured him piously, he assured me he greatly respected the WRNS, but he had to find his enemy. Gradually he calmed down. By the time the CO emerged, I was able to introduce them to each other (I was a little embarrassed by his conviction by this time that I was the CO). We all shook hands and eventually he departed in peace, still reiterating his respect for the WRNS. The incident was never mentioned to me again. My roommate was out for dinner that night; none of the other officers spoke of what had happened.

For the first few weeks at the Ministry of Aircraft Production, I was convinced that the navy and I had made a mistake – I did not have the technical knowledge and would never be able to do the work satisfactorily. I was part of a tiny department called RDE(N), Research and Development of Engines (Naval). In my office there were three of us, a pleasant but almost totally silent lieutenant, myself (Third Officer, Air Engineer) and a clerk, a civil servant of many years' experience, to whom I became deeply indebted for her help in understanding at least the way the paper trail worked. She was always helpful and treated me with (undeserved) respect. Just down the passage was the rest of the department, a young Captain and a Lieutenant Commander. The rest of the big multi-storey building was full of boffins (civil servants) and Royal Air Force personnel. My main task was to read and comment on a flow of files, each dealing with an episode in which the engine of a Fleet Air Arm plane had failed in some way, often but not always leading to a crash. Sometimes, needing better understanding of some feature of the engine, I would seek out one of the technically knowledgeable boffins; they too were very good to me, and would explain patiently, sometimes leading me through the intricacies of a blueprint. 'Blueprint' had been just a word to me; I had never seen one before this time. I was sure my predecessor, with whom I had had the briefest of overlaps, had studied them in kindergarten. I was certainly right that she had much more knowledge than I had. I believe she had worked before the war for an aircraft manufacturer, and in addition was a qualified pilot. Later, when I left, I learnt that the boffins had found her intimidating and hard to work with. Much later, I have wondered whether she really was unduly pushy, or whether her difficulties were a manifestation of anti-feminist misogyny, a response to her exceptional abilities and qualifications. Then, I was simply grateful for their help, always tendered with respect, never with condescension. What we were looking for was any pattern that might emerge in a particular model of engine, suggesting a design flaw, or pointing to a possible useful modification. We also discussed various developments (the lieutenant could break silence for this) and any interesting news that crossed our desks. Occasionally we had an opportunity to leave the office: once, the lieutenant drove me down in his exciting little sports car (what a surprise!) to see an exhibition of captured German aircraft. On another occasion we made a trip for a special viewing of the first jet engine powered military planes, which only came into production in mid-1944, closely following similar development in Germany. The airfield at which the demonstration was held had a grass runway; I remember seeing the grass catch on fire behind the plane as it revved up for takeoff.

At one point we found ourselves confronted by a series of several disastrous engine failures in a new engine, the Bristol Taurus, a rotary engine with a sleeve valve, an efficient engine valve but one that was proving subject to what we called 'hydraulicing' (Wikipedia has it as hydraulic locking). Hydraulicing can be described as a peak example of an irresistible force meeting an immovable object. Without going into details, the oil was finding a way to pool in the sleeve channel, without any way of getting out, so that when the rotating sleeve descended, something had to give, and the whole thing broke up. I was sent off to Bristol Aircraft Works (in Bristol) to take a three-week course on the Taurus engine.

The course was interesting, but the circumstances were difficult for me, and I am sure I ought to have been able to handle them better. I was the only woman student, the only officer, and one of only two members of the navy; the other was a highly experienced and qualified Master-at-Arms. All the other students were from the Royal Air Force, all had years of experience. The real crunch was that all had worked on Hercules rotary engines; my hands-on experience had been entirely with the in-line Merlin engine. No more than a mere smattering of knowledge from the few hours spent on the old model Hercules engine at *Fledgling* remained with me, and except for a very general knowledge of the difficulties arising with the Taurus itself, my work at MAP had done nothing to supplement this. The course was well designed, with a wonderful set of diagrams of the working of the sleeve valve, but little about the accessory components of the engine, unchanged from previous rotary types. The instructor would pick up a large chunk of metal and say, 'Oh, you know all about this – just the same as on the old Herc', and set it down again (I guess that was the carburettor? I would be thinking). I did not have the courage to explain my problem to the instructor, who was always surrounded by a companionable group of fellow men during any break, and my fellow students avoided me. I asked a few questions, but only on topics familiar enough that I could do so without making a fool of myself. So I remained visibly standoffish and – even more painfully – stupid. I was in fact learning a great deal, studying the diagrams and the manual and gaining a comfortable grasp of the sleeve valve and of the overall engine. But the test would include a great deal of detail that was unfamiliar to me, and my bumbling had been apparent. It never occurred to anyone – including me – that the solution might lie in a couple of short sessions of special instruction. Someone found a way out that was charitable – or condescending – and worked for them though really not for me; at the end of the course I was told that officers did not take tests. In some ways that was the worst possible solution for me; I had as good a grasp as anyone of the working of the essential new features of the Taurus, and might have been able to show this on a test.

My accommodation provided me with no relief. I remember no details of the naval quarters where I was billeted, except that I was alone almost all the time. I do recall that it was the only time I ever had a 'bat-woman', that common adjunct of officerdom; she shined my shoes, and I think she made my bed, the whole done silently and efficiently in about fifteen minutes. I was provided with a sandwich lunch (which I ate alone) and some kind of breakfast and dinner at the quarters; I am almost sure I ate these alone too. Certainly I found no opportunity to relate the experiences of the day and find the gems of humour they contained.

When I went back to MAP, I was somewhat burdened by my sense that I had confirmed all the stereotypes of women's technical incompetence, and failed to reflect credit on my position. Yet I was aware that I had acquired the knowledge I had been sent to get, that I now thoroughly understood how a sleeve valve worked. I had an underlying sense that perhaps it hadn't all been my fault. But I knew I should have been able to handle it better.

On August 6, the Allies dropped the first atomic bomb on Hiroshima, and three days later, another on Nagasaki. On August 14, Japan surrendered. Much later, teaching twentieth-century history, and exposed to research by colleagues in the Peace History Society, I learnt that Japan had not needed this atrocity to bring her to the point of negotiation. Like many others, I came to some realisation of quite how terrible was this new weapon, seeing a grainy film shot on the day of the Hiroshima bomb, and learning, more gradually, of the long-lasting effects. From time to time, we at MAP had seen photographs not generally released, of the devastation caused by the carpet-bombing of European cities. I could not get my mind around something that was in fact exponentially worse than this. Even then, I felt sick at heart. And on August 7, I had a phone call from Peter T, saying only, 'Now you know what I have been working on'. The Cavendish Laboratory in Oxford, where Peter worked, had taken part in the development of the bomb.

Now the war was really over, and the government set to work to demobilise its huge military services. A government circular that came through the office regularly began to contain lists of the service numbers of those whose demobilisation was coming up. At first the process was slow, and I did not study the list carefully – until suddenly one day, glancing at an issue of a couple of weeks previous, I saw my number and my category. The lieutenant was not there that day, so I went along the corridor to the Lieutenant Commander, who greeted me kindly and asked whether I was there to request a promotion, indicating that he thought that a reasonable expectation. 'No,' I said, 'I seem to have been demobilised last month'. He and the captain were not much taken aback; they did not have to let me go while there was work for me to do, and I was gratified to find that they thought me indispensable at least for the time being. Conscious that I had no job to go to, I was in no hurry to leave. Shortly afterwards, I was asked to stay on, with a new three-year contract, binding on both sides. I had enjoyed my work, and had scant skill in other fields, but I don't think I hesitated: I was sickened with war and could not contemplate uniformed service in peacetime. I refused the offer, but was glad to stay on meanwhile. I needed some time to think about other possibilities in this new, unfamiliar world.

A few weeks later, Second Officer Etty-Leal reappeared, willing and more than qualified to take back the job, and I was ready to leave. I was directed to some demob centre where I was issued with a demob civvy suit (coat and skirt) some coupons and a new duffel bag. My one big triumph was that I also managed to bring away my beloved wooden toolbox and its contents.

Epilogue

A curious interlude followed the end of the war. My memories of this time are clouded by a sense of unreality, and I have no clear idea of chronology. My parents, rather unexpectedly and perhaps unwisely, moved back into Mount View. A gardener, digging away at a high pile of earth where a bomb had fallen, showed me a daffodil bulb that had sent off its usual spring shoot to find the light. Finding instead more and more displaced soil, it had reduced itself to a single pale stem and had pushed on inch by inch until it reached daylight. Only the last five inches of its eight-foot-long shoot had turned green in the sun, there could be no flower. For me, a symbol of loss and of hope.

Ever since the heavy bombing had levelled the streets I had grown up with, I had observed that, living and working far away, the back of my mind had not fully internalised the permanence of the material damage. Irrational as I knew it to be, I would find myself thinking that once the war was over, things would be as they had been before the war. I knew I was changed, and mostly it was only the physical landscape that my fragmentary delusion applied to, but when I thought of shopping, my mind would be walking along George Street, from Pophams to Dingles to Yeos to Spooners, all familiar department stores. For years after, I occasionally had to make a conscious effort to be in touch with reality. Now, in the teens of the twenty-first century, I see images of incomparable complete devastation in cities like Aleppo, and I can feel a shadow of the pain and confusion that comes from the destruction of those objects to which one's childhood memories look for substance. I cannot come near to being with the pain of the loss of the people who trod those streets.

George came home at last from India, much older, oh, so much older than the boy who had left us nearly five years before. Douglas and Lorraine were reunited for only a short time before his demobilisation was postponed – a bitter blow – and he was sent off with the occupying forces to Austria for another year. George and I were lucky to have Mount View as a home in which to regroup, the same but very different. My bedroom was little changed, but his was equipped with no less than three superfluous shower stalls. Nannie, the same loving, stabilising influence – and a great cook – was still with us, and for a time her mother, unable to live alone in her cottage any more, was there too.

Here and there we captured fleeting fragments of our destroyed youth, looking for some continuity between the past and the new normal. The all over linoleum floor covering was great for dancing, but we only managed to organise that once or twice. We met up again with our prewar friends, and missed those who were no longer alive. We invited friends for tennis, and George argued angrily with our mother about the propriety of telling guests to bring their own sandwiches for tea. Bread was rationed in this postwar England as it had never been during the war – much more of a hardship in working families than it was in ours, but my mother was offended at the idea of having guests if we could not provide for them.

We went again to dances at the Moorland Links; my principal partner, Ralph Davison, was now a tall good-looking career officer in the Royal Marines and we danced together often. George brought for a long visit a fellow engineer, a former colleague in India and now paralysed from the waist down. At his request we set him up, in the rather splendid and under used dining room, with a telescope to gaze out over Plymouth to the sea and exercise his considerable skill in identifying vessels. He and George allowed for no gloom, but kept us laughing with their recounting of episodes from their service.

Another highlight was a trip with George in his newly purchased second-hand MG sports car, imbued with more glamour than comfort. I remember a long night journey in pouring rain throughout which I worked the defective windscreen wiper by hand, under a more-or-less rainproof hood. We visited evangelical cousins in Essex, finding their young people earnestly converting children on the sands of Clacton, and we visited the ageing cousins in Hampshire.

Short of clothes in those still-rationed days, I would not ordinarily wear the uniform I was still temporarily entitled to. Yet I yielded once and wore it to attend a celebratory service at Plymouth Citadel with my mother, and found myself swept again briefly into some kind of patriotic fervour. I do not grudge my mother the pleasure that gave her. But I was conflicted and ambivalent; I never applied for the minor war service medals I had earned.

Nor did I go back to the Quaker Meeting, feeling myself unworthy and besmirched – in that context. So many conflicting emotions. Loss, some pride in my still unusual technical knowledge, memories of deep friendships forged among the hardships of life on the air station, an overwhelming realisation that I had been privileged with experiences that would never have come my way without the war.

I don't think that either George or I had any wholehearted wish to pick up just where we had left off in September 1939. For a while we were wandering rather aimlessly, while we found our new directions. Perhaps George had more helpful discussion, especially with our father, than I had. The evangelical cousin in Hampshire made a tempting offer to teach him to farm and make him his heir, but this was weighed and rejected. Finally, he delighted my father by seeking work with the Church Missionary Society, and after training, he became a lay administrator in Nigeria.

I did not really find anyone to talk with about what route I should take. It wasn't even worth looking for openings where I could use my Fleet Air Arm experience in a peace context. I might have unusual expertise in air mechanics – for a woman – but you didn't have to be sexist to recognise that the scant jobs in any related field would be being sought by hundreds, if not thousands, of men more knowledgeable than I.

What other skills, qualifications and experience did I have?

I don't know, to this day, what direction I would have taken if there had been no war. I had, not unreasonably, not formulated any clear career plans before going to university, though I was leaning towards some form of social service, whatever that meant. I don't think now that the general direction of my thinking was altered by the war. I had been moving towards socialism and concern for social justice for several years, profoundly influenced by parts of my Downe House education. The war had given me valuable experience, but had separated me from any further academic or practical training of relevance.

I now looked rather wistfully at the opportunities there were to help refugees (then known as 'displaced persons'), or to help in distressed war-torn Europe. If I had any sense of a 'calling', this was probably it, but I lacked confidence, the right connections or much in the way of expertise for this kind of work, and I scarcely even knew how to apply. I had a small amount of experience in teaching, and a good degree. I began to take the *Times Education* and *Higher Education* supplements regularly and scan the job ads carefully. There were not many openings, but two proved fruitful, and my spirits began to rise. One was as a tutor at a small private post-secondary school for young women (it called itself a 'Club') in London, focused mainly on the study of politics and current political institutions. I think I recognised it as a sensible alternative, for politically minded well-to-do parents of young daughters, to the customary vacuous round of debutante social life. I did not until later suspect that it might be more of an institution for the education of politicians' wives than for female politicians. I don't know, now, which it was closer to. I liked the idea of working with very small groups, being closely involved with what was going on, visiting the House of Commons frequently, and furthering my own understanding. At the interview, I volunteered the information that I was a socialist, not wanting to hide what might be a deal-breaker, and was appropriately (and kindly) told that I really should not have found it necessary to spell that out. And it was not held against me: a few days later, I was offered the job.

At the same time, increasingly, I had begun to think how good it would be to be away from Britain for a few years, to distance myself and to make a new start in a less weary land. Before I had made a decision about the London job offer, I was called for an interview under the auspices of – of all things – the Society for the Overseas Settlement of British Women, a body created to help find opportunities for women after the First World War. The term 'surplus women' was never spoken, but I suppose that was what I was and what I felt like. I was rather drawn to Canada, but there were no openings. I was interviewed by Miss LeMaitre, Principal of Roedean School, Johannesburg, who was in the UK to recruit teachers to fill a number of vacancies in a school whose name identified it as on a par in the spectrum of elitism (but also I could hope in educational quality) with my own school – would I never get away from my privileged background? But I liked Miss LeMaitre, and I accepted a three-year contract to teach English, minor as were my qualifications in this subject.

Preparations and farewells kept me busy. My father was very sad, my mother excited for me, Nannie made me two lovely everyday dresses from Liberty cottons just making their postwar reappearance. My dance partner, Ralph, was more upset than I had expected.

Nannie and my father drove me to Southampton to embark on a Castle liner. The *Carnarvon Castle* had barely been rehabilitated from its war service as a troopship and accommodation for the sixteen-day voyage (yes, you knew you were making a big move in those days) was Spartan. All the women were in two-tier bunks in large cabins, all the men were far below decks in what were known as standees. No special arrangements were made for a few honeymoon couples, who were faced with a trip far from the romantic sea cruise they may have anticipated. Men and women even ate at separate sittings. A handful of what had been first-class cabins was occupied by some unnamed distinguished travellers, but they wisely kept out of sight.

Sitting space on the decks was reserved by getting up in time to put down your blanket where there would be some shade. I became

188

The Carnavon Castle

acquainted with two other teachers going to Roedean. I took part in crossing-the-equator ceremonies, and in organised deck sports where I talked a young man into partnering me in a three-legged race. Coached by me – it was a skill of my youth – we won a small tote bag. My good sea legs sustained me through the Bay of Biscay, although many of the other thirty-five occupants of our cabin – and of course the children were with the women, not with the men – were not so fortunate.

For me the trip was no hardship. In some ways it felt like an adventure, especially when shoals of flying fish broke through the surface of the ocean. But in some ways it seemed a continuation of the constrained experience of wartime – until one day the magic broke through. We had a scheduled stop at the island of Madeira, but as we approached we were warned that there was no certainty that we would be allowed ashore. The *Carnarvon Castle* looked like a troopship to the folk of Madeira, and they had not enjoyed the visits of crowds of troops. However, they were persuaded that we were closer to prewar tourists than to troops, and might indeed present a needed chance of some income.

We drew in to the harbour as light faded. We would go ashore the next day, but it is that first evening that stays with me. The air was warm and moist; lights shone all up the hillside on shore, and soon there were lights on the water all around us, carried by small boats bearing all kinds of things to sell. Divers dived for coins, bargains were made, baskets were lowered down with money and pulled up again with fruit, beautifully embroidered cloths, local handwork of all kinds. After the austerity of Britain, for me it was not just exotic, it was sheer magic. I shook off much of the sadness of war and found myself facing forward once more, with anticipation and hope. It would be a while before I felt a clear sense of direction again, longer still before I found my way back to Quakers. But I felt young again and South Africa had much to teach me. There were people to meet, mountains to climb and political issues to address.